RETRIEVING THE AMERICAN PAST

1920-1970

2001 Advanced Placement Edition

PEARSON CUSTOM PUBLISHING

Director of Database Publishing: Michael Payne
Acquisitions Editor: Ellen M. Kuhl
Editor: Colby R. Lawrence
Marketing: Hester Tinti-Kane, Nathan L. Wilbur
Operations Manager: Eric M. Kenney

Cover Art: Christie's Images, Long Island City, NY
Granger Collection, New York, NY
Superstock, Jacksonville, FL
Tony Stone Images, Chicago, IL

Printed in the United States of America

10 9 8 7 6 5 4 3 2 1

0-536-62209-4
BA 5567

PEARSON CUSTOM PUBLISHING
75 Arlington Street, Suite #300/Boston, MA 02116
Pearson Education Group

CONTRIBUTORS

Senior Editors
Michael Les Benedict
Mark Grimsley
Susan M. Hartmann
Margaret E. Newell
Carla Gardina Pestana
Leila J. Rupp
David L. Stebenne
Warren R. Van Tine

Current Managing Editor
John Day Tully

Assistant Managing Editor
Pamela E. Pennock

Copy Editor
Ann Heiss

Contributing Editors

Tyler Anbinder
Kenneth J. Andrien
Jean Harvey Baker
Michael Les Benedict
Mansel Blackford
Paul C. Bowers
Rowland Brucken
John D. Buenker
John C. Burnham
Joan E. Cashin
William R. Childs
Albert J. Churella
Steven Conn
Saul Cornell
Jeanette Davis
Merton L. Dillon
Daniel Feller
Charles Coleman Finlay
Mark Grimsley
Bernard N. Grindel
Peter L. Hahn
Susan M. Hartmann
Mary Ann Heiss
Earl J. Hess
Michael J. Hogan

Bruce Karhoff
Terence Kehoe
K. Austin Kerr
James McCaffrey
Allan R. Millett
Pamela J. Mills
Daniel Nelson
Margaret E. Newell
Josef Ostyn
Carla Gardina Pestana
Patrick D. Reagan
Randolph A. Roth
John A. M. Rothney
Leila J. Rupp
Richard D. Shiels
David Sicilia
C. Edward Skeen
Amy L. S. Staples
David L. Stebenne
David Steigerwald
Marshall F. Stevenson, Jr.
Warren R. Van Tine
Christopher Waldrep
J. Samuel Walker

PREFACE TO THE 2001 ADVANCED PLACEMENT EDITION OF *RETRIEVING THE AMERICAN PAST*

To help you prepare for your Advanced Placement American history exam, *Retrieving the American Past* offers you a variety of topics and sources culled from twentieth century American history and historical scholarship. *Retrieving the American Past* is a customizable history reader that allows the college-level instructor to select chapters from more than seventy topics for classroom discussion and analysis. In the college edition, each chapter offers a choice of secondary and primary sources that, together, enable students to understand and perform the complex tasks of historical analysis and interpretation. This winning combination of flexibility and comprehensiveness that has propelled *Retrieving the American Past* to the top of the college textbook market is now available to you, the student of Advanced Placement American history.

The chapters included in this special edition have been carefully chosen for the 2001 AP exam. In May of 2000, the College Board announced that the Documents Based Question (DBQ) for the 2001 exam would concern a historically significant issue from the time period 1920–1970. Accordingly, the editorial board of *Retrieving the American Past*, in consultation with AP teachers and graders, selected seven chapters for this edition that individually address some of the most important issues of the period and collectively offer a broad and varied look at the concerns driving the historical profession. You will find the more traditional subjects of diplomacy and politics, as well as newer areas of inquiry such as race, gender, and class. This edition covers topics such as advertising, the origins of the Cold War, and the civil rights movement. Together, these chapters cover possible topics for the DBQ, indicate the different types of primary sources that the DBQ may include, and, in two cases, serve as models for how primary sources are incorporated into historical analysis

All of the chapters in this edition of *Retrieving the American Past* contain primary sources, but the first two—"Advertising and Marketing in American Society During the 1920s and 1930s" and "The Expulsion and Relocation of Japanese Americans in World War II"—also include secondary sources. Secondary sources are accounts written by historians in which they interpret the period in question. Primary source documents are the evidence from a period on which historians base their interpretations. They can be diaries, letters, essays, newspaper articles, political cartoons, maps, and other written or visual materials that were created in the historical time period under investigation. In the chapter "Advertising and Marketing in American Society During the 1920s and 1930s," for example, the secondary sources offer historical arguments on the place and function of advertising in American society. The primary sources include images and contemporary accounts from the 1920s and 1930s that enable you to evaluate these arguments.

For the Documents Based Question, think of yourself as an historian writing a secondary source based on the primary sources provided. Using these fragments of the past and your outside knowledge, you must fashion an historical interpretation that acknowledges and makes sense of the evidence. The first two chapters of *Retrieving the American Past* include secondary sources as well as primary sources so that you can observe how historians interrogate primary sources and fit them into larger interpretive structures. You should also notice how historians read the same document in different ways, and perhaps more important, how they argue their positions. As you approach each primary source document, consider the time period in which it was written or created, its origins and authorship, its audience (both intended and unintended), and its point of view. Consider what each source tells you about the historical period, and engage in some "reading between the lines" to discern more concealed meanings. After you have thought carefully about the primary sources, practice constructing an historical argument based upon them. Your successful response to a DBQ will not only incorporate the documents into a sensible narrative, it will also use them, along with your outside knowledge of the subject, as support for your interpretation.

Contents

Advertising and Marketing in American Society During the 1920s and 1930s

Albert J. Churella

INTRODUCTION

The years between 1880 and 1920 marked a period of profound change in the United States. Millions of immigrants entered the country, while millions of rural Americans moved to cities—both groups adjusting to the rapid pace of urban life. Railroads and telegraph lines knit the country together, allowing for rapid and reliable transportation and communication. In many industries, business firms grew to a massive size, producing vast quantities of steel, oil, chemicals, and agricultural products.

All of these developments helped to set the stage for an advertising and marketing revolution during the 1920s and 1930s. Although advertising and marketing are often seen as identical to one another, the two concepts are actually quite different. Marketing, the more inclusive term, refers to the efforts of a seller to exchange goods or services for money by developing new or improved products, implementing price structures, packaging these products, distributing them to the consumer, and making consumers aware of the products' existence through advertising. Advertising, only one component of marketing, uses print, radio, or other media to deliver simple repetitive messages emphasizing certain virtues of a particular product.

Before the American Industrial Revolution of the late 1800s, advertising had been primarily descriptive in nature. Ads simply stated that certain items were available at a particular price, and rarely mentioned whether or not these products would produce any benefits for the consumer. Patent medicine advertisements were considerably different, however. Around the turn of the century, many firms concocted patent "medicines" that usually did little more than provide temporary pain relief—probably because most contained potent combinations of alcohol and narcotics. Manufacturers, however, issued lavish color ads, claiming that these medicines cured virtually every disease. Such obviously fraudulent claims discredited advertising in general, since the public assumed that only worthless products needed to be advertised.

The First World War redeemed the power of advertising. President Wilson established the Committee on Public Information (CPI), a federal government agency responsible for encouraging popular support for the war effort. CPI ads, often prepared by commercial advertising agencies, blanketed the country and proved quite effective at whipping up anti-German feelings. The success of these ads persuaded many manufacturers to take another look at the advertising issue.

Other factors contributed to the rapid growth of advertising during the 1920s. The rise of American big business created a large group of managers, engineers, and scientists, and this new middle class possessed both the money and the leisure time necessary to enjoy consumer products. Many companies, having saturated the market for producers' goods (such as steel and oil), began to manufacture a truly incredible variety of consumer goods. Technological and manufacturing advances brought refrigerators, automobiles, radios, and other consumer goods within the reach of middle-class and working-class buyers. Trains allowed identical consumer products to be placed on store shelves throughout the United States. National circulation magazines, such as the Ladies' Home Journal, McCall's, and the Saturday Evening Post, enabled manufacturers to reach an enormous audience. Advances in color printing technology enabled many ads to appear in color—far more effective than a black-and-white ad. As chain stores (smaller versions of modern supermarkets) like A&P replaced "mom and pop" groceries, consumers could no longer rely on the clerk behind the counter to provide advice on which products best suited their needs. Instead, shoppers frequently relied on labels, on national brand names, and on the advertisements they had just seen in a magazine or heard on the radio.

The advertising and consumer goods explosion that character-ized the 1920s gave enormous power to advertising and marketing executives—the power to shape, or at least to influence, public opinion. Advertising and marketing executives tended to be young, well-educated, upper-middle class, and almost always male—this despite the fact that women made 75 percent of all consumer purchases. Ads reflected the demographic characteristics of ad writers, and most ads depicted middle-class, white, young professionals and their children. African Americans and other minorities rarely appeared, and even then were often por-trayed in subservient roles—as a janitor or railroad sleeping car porter, for example. Even though working-class Americans out-numbered middle-class Americans, the former group rarely ap-peared in ads.

Advertisers, it seems, exhibited both contempt and compas-sion for the American people. Ad writers often felt that the average American consumer was ignorant, badly dressed, unschooled in even the most basic social graces, and unaware of the vast and wonderful possibilities of consumerism. On the other hand, ad writers often exhibited compassion for these same prospective consumers, believing that all of their problems could be solved if they purchased the proper consumer goods. Advertisers insisted that they were not simply selling products, they were making consumers healthier, happier, and more successful. Advertisers even attempted to reconcile a basic tension between capitalism (which invariably concentrates wealth in the hands of a few) and democracy (which emphasizes the fundamental concept that "all men are created equal"). Ad writers did so through the idea of the "democracy of goods," which stressed that all people were essen-tially made equal through the products (goods) that they con-sumed, regardless of their level of income. At a time when some Americans—and even more Europeans—felt that socialism or communism constituted viable alternatives to capitalism, the de-mocracy of goods offered the promise of a peaceful and harmonious reconciliation between America's democratic ideals and the unde-niable class stratification of 1920s society. The poor need not envy the rich (nor challenge their elite economic, political, and social status) because rich and poor alike could enjoy the same mass-produced benefits of capitalism. A bit naïve, perhaps, but at least indicative of the advertisers' desire to help create what they perceived as a better society.

THE ROLE OF ADVERTISING IN AMERICAN SOCIETY

Almost everyone agrees that advertising has had a significant impact on the American consumer culture. Considerable debate has emerged, however, over the exact nature of advertising's influence. Some historians argue that advertising executives and business leaders engaged in a near conspiracy designed to force Americans to buy consumer products. These scholars feel that advertising has warped American society by downplaying such important issues as class conflict (the rich vs. the poor, or managers vs. workers); that advertising has forced Americans to work long and hard simply to purchase items that they do not need. They further assert that advertisers are able to transform wants into needs and luxuries into necessities, in the process wasting natural resources, polluting the environment, and widening the gap between the "haves" and the "have-nots."

Other scholars regard advertising as much less pervasive and threatening. They argue that advertising merely reflects long-term changes in American society; in other words, advertisers see no value in writing ads unless people have already demonstrated a desire to own a new product. Ads may cause consumers to buy car "A" rather than car "B" but still have no impact on the consumers' initial decision to purchase some type of car. Exploitation of natural resources and rampant consumerism may indeed exist, they explain, but these often unfortunate trends are part of a natural human desire to acquire more "stuff" and are not the responsibility of advertisements or of advertisers.

The Crisco Story

Crisco is not only a familiar product found in grocery stores throughout the world; it also provides an example of a stunningly successful market- ing campaign, one that set the pattern for others during the 1920s, 1930s, and later. This excerpt shows that Procter and Gamble did not develop Crisco to meet a consumer need (actual or anticipated), but rather to increase the efficiency and profitability of their other manufac- turing enterprises. Once Procter and Gamble had developed Crisco, the challenge became to convince consumers that they actually needed a product that they had always done without and had never known they wanted. Excerpted from Susan Strasser, Satisfaction Guaranteed: The Making of the American Mass Market *(New York, 1989), 3-5, 9-15.*

In January of 1912, the Procter and Gamble Company of Cincinnati, Ohio, introduced Crisco, a solid vegetable shortening that it described to the readers of the *Ladies' Home Journal* and at least four other popular national magazines as "An Absolutely New Product, A Scientific Discovery Which will Affect Every Kitchen in America." . . .

. . . The experiments that produced Crisco had begun in 1905, supported by capital from Procter and Gamble's several success- ful brands of soap, including the well-known Ivory. In part, the research was an attempt to generate a product that would assure P & G its supply of cottonseed oil, which it was already using to make soap. . . . By creating and marketing new products that used large quantities of cottonseed oil, Procter and Gamble could achieve not only financial growth but a more powerful position in purchasing its raw materials. For five years, under top-secret conditions, the laboratories worked to solve the technical difficul- ties of producing an all-vegetable solid fat in commercial quanti- ties. In 1910, they achieved a patentable product. . . .

At the end of April 1911, the company's executive committee met in William Procter's office to vote on the name and the label

Excerpts reprinted from *Satisfaction Guaranteed: The Making of the American Mass Market,* by Susan Strasser, Pantheon Books. Copyright © 1989 by Susan Strasser.

design. They approved a package incorporating the company's moon-and-stars logo and substituted "Crisco" for "Krispo," a name they had adopted the month before, but on which a Chicago cracker manufacturer had a prior claim. They then turned the product over to Stanley Resor, who had left Procter and Collier, the company's own advertising agency, to establish a Cincinnati office for J. Walter Thompson. Resor assigned copywriting responsibility to Helen Lansdowne, the woman he was later to marry and with whom he would acquire both financial and administrative control of this major New York advertising firm; Lansdowne would become the first woman in the Advertising Hall of Fame. Procter and Gamble was so concerned about marketing Crisco that the board of directors for the first time opened its meetings to a woman. Five times during 1911, Lansdowne took the train from New York to Cincinnati to represent the agency and "answer questions from the woman's point of view."

Product testing continued, now outside the company laboratories. University-based food researchers received samples for testing and recipe development; the company later quoted these scientists and home economists, testifying to Crisco's purity and goodness. The product made its first public appearance at a summer party for P & G employees. Like the Cincinnati clubwomen who soon began attending "Crisco teas," the workers carried home full-sized (one-and-a-half-pound) samples of the product. In October, Cincinnati's Burnet House Hotel and Queen City Club adopted the shortening; they were eventually followed by Chesapeake and Ohio Railway dining cars and New York City's Lüchow's Restaurant. During these tests, the company continued to refine the product, altering the formula in response to complaints that it went rancid.

Meanwhile, Resor and Lansdowne tested seven or eight different sales-promotion plans simultaneously. In one city, they tried newspaper advertising; in another, nothing but streetcar ads or outdoor posters or store demonstrations. In some cities, house-to-house canvassers sold the product; in others, salesmen courted retailers in conjunction with a house-to-house campaign. A specially hired staff worked on a more general analysis of the shortening market, investigating the competition and the uses of various products.

In December of 1911, a month before the first national advertising, the company sent packages containing three to six full-sized cans to every grocer in the United States, with a letter describing the forthcoming campaign. "We want you to have Crisco in stock, so that you can supply the first demand this advertising will create among your customers," one such letter read. "Sell the six cans, and then order what further supply you need from your jobber." "Crisco is being placed in the grocery stores as rapidly as possible," the January magazine ad told the grocers' customers. "If your own grocer does not yet keep it, you probably will find it in one of the other stores in your neighborhood." For the first few months, shoppers who failed to obtain Crisco through the stores could buy a package (but only one) direct from Procter and Gamble, for twenty-five cents and the name of the offending grocer. By the end of 1915, the company could report in a *Saturday Evening Post* advertisement that "through the length and breadth of the country, in big stores and little, Crisco is now a staple."

During those first four years, the company promoted Crisco extensively and continuously, not only advertising in national magazines but enlisting grocer support. Cooperating storekeepers wrote letters to their charge customers, enclosing booklets about the shortening and offering to add Crisco to the delivery order. "Just let us send you a small package today on our recommendation," a Dallas form letter read. "Then see if it doesn't change completely your ideas of fried foods." A Rochester, New York merchant sent his letter on a printed folder supplied by the company, picturing a black cook displaying a plateful of biscuits. "We have seldom had anything that has met with such immediate success," he wrote.

For several years, six Crisco demonstrators toured cities throughout the country from September through June, conducting week-long cooking schools. The schools were paid for by Procter and Gamble, arranged for by a P & G advance man, and cosponsored by local newspapers, which lent their names to the schools—the "*Herald* Cooking School"—and their columns to the new product. A pseudonymous writer for the Fort Smith, Arkansas *Southwest American*, for example, was much taken by demonstrator Mrs. Kate B. Vaughn, "a perfect dear" and a "woman's woman" who served her audience peas, lamb chops, potato nests, white cake, marshmallow pudding, and baking-powder biscuits. "Mrs. Vaughn used a new shortening for these biscuits and told why she used it," the writer declared, "all of which caused me to stop in at my grocer's and purchase a can of the stuff, which I tried with great success last night."

In its 1913 prospectus for newspaper publishers, the company asserted that the demonstrators downplayed product promotion. Although they did discuss Crisco, their lectures covered other topics as well. "For, if women believed the lecture was there merely to promote or advertise a trademarked article, they would not be so apt to come a second time," the company told the publishers. "The audience may or may not, however, believe that the manufacturer of Crisco remunerates the lecturer in some way for the endorsement she gives the product." Given that the endorsement involved handing out full-sized samples and Crisco recipe pamphlets, only the credulous would believe otherwise.

These pamphlets, illustrated with pictures of the demonstrators, published the results of a continuous process of recipe development that also enabled Procter and Gamble to furnish cookbooks through the mail. By June 1912, consumers could write for *Tested Crisco Recipes*, a free paperback with a hundred recipes and "the interesting story of Crisco's discovery and manufacture." Late in 1913, a new book appeared: *The Story of Crisco*, in a complimentary version with 250 recipes, and in a clothbound "quality edition" available for five 2-cent stamps. The latter, *A Calendar of Dinners*, suggesting 365 menus with 615 recipes, went through at least twenty-six editions by 1925. These books supplemented the company's other cooking instructions. Recipes appeared in Crisco advertising as early as April 1912, and an eight-page, circle-shaped recipe booklet was packed inside the lid of every can.

Other packaging innovations aimed the product at particular markets. Soon after a special ten-pound container was created for their compact dining-car kitchens, twenty-two railroads adopted Crisco. Another special package, advertised in the Yiddish media and sold in Jewish neighborhoods, bore the seals of Rabbi Lifsitz of Cincinnati and Rabbi Margolies of New York, who pronounced the contents kosher. Margolies, according to *The Story of Crisco*, "said that the Hebrew Race had been waiting 4,000 years for Crisco." By enabling immigrant cooks to bake American pie without lard, Crisco joined the forces of Americanization, a movement that enlisted many home economists and social workers who hoped to transform foreigners through their eating habits.

At the end of the first year of Crisco marketing, J. George Frederick, former editor of the widely read advertising industry weekly *Printers' Ink,* wrote that the campaign had established a new standard for modern marketing. In a *Printers' Ink* article entitled "Efficient Planning Before Advertising," he described the testing procedures, infusing his prose with the popular jargon of efficiency and scientific management. "Instead of filling the earth and the sky and all that therein is with flashes of publicity and grand hurrah," he maintained, Procter and Gamble "has in a final and authoritative manner indicated the maximum efficiency method of marketing and finding distribution for a new product."

The methods were not quite final; over the next seventy-five years, marketers developed more sophisticated techniques that employed technologies and systems undreamed of in 1912. Nonetheless, both the Crisco publicity and the campaign planning look strikingly modern. Today's marketers employ many of the same general planning principles and promotional techniques, although they apply them to television commercials and rely on computer-analyzed statistics. The testing and refining of the product formula, label, and marketing strategy continue, for Crisco and for other successful consumer products. The kosher packages and the dining-car marketing provide evidence of what is now called market segmentation and product positioning, with special packages, product formulas, and marketing campaigns aimed at particular groups of potential buyers. Late-twentieth-century consumers still receive free samples and read recipe suggestions in magazine advertising. And although little record remains of the Crisco teas, they probably sounded much like the focus groups that contemporary marketers convene.

Does Advertising Reflect Society or Distort It?

Advertisers frequently argue that their ads merely reflect existing social values and needs; that they only promote products and services that people know they want. While historian Roland Marchand does not believe that advertisers conspiratorially manipulate society, he does suggest that ads have selected and sorted; in other words, that advertisers chose a very narrow range of lifestyles and portrayed these as representative of the experiences of all Americans, regardless of gender, race, class, or occupation. Excerpted from Roland Marchand, Advertising the American Dream: Making Way for Modernity, 1920-1940 *(Berkeley, 1985), xvi-xvii, xxi, 1-2, 4, 359, 87, 264, 116, 217-18, 220, 285, 318, 300, 288, 290-91, 337.*

I cannot prove conclusively that the American people absorbed the values and ideas of the ads, nor that consumers wielded the power to ensure that the ads would mirror their lives. In fact, as advertisers quickly perceived, people did not usually want ads to reflect themselves, their immediate social relationships, or their broader society exactly. They wanted not a true mirror but a Zerrspiegel, a distorting mirror that would enhance certain images. Even the term Zerrspiegel, denoting a fun-house mirror, fails to suggest fully the scope of advertising distortions of reality. Such a mirror distorts the shapes of the objects it reflects, but it nevertheless provides some image of everything within its field of vision. Advertising's mirror not only distorted, it also selected. Some social realities hardly appeared at all. One has to search diligently in the ads of the 1920s and 1930s to find even fleeting glimpses of such common scenes as religious services, factory workers on the job, sports fans enjoying a boxing match or baseball game, or working-class families at home.

The angle of refraction, and hence the degree of distortion of these advertising images, was determined not only by the efforts of advertisers to respond to consumers' desires for fantasy and wish-fulfillment but also by a variety of other factors. The most obvious source of distortion in advertising's mirror was the presumption by advertisers that the public preferred an image of "life as it ought to be, life in the millennium" to an image of literal reality. "The people are seeking to escape from themselves," concluded a writer in *Advertising and Selling* in 1926. "They want to live in a more exciting world." Working under this assumption, ad creators tried to reflect public aspirations rather than contemporary circumstances, to mirror popular fantasies rather than social realities. Advertisers recognized that consumers would rather identify with scenes of higher status than ponder reflections of their actual lives. In response, they often sought to give products a "class image" by placing them in what recent advertising jargon would call "upscale" settings.

Even apart from such upscale strategies, advertisements of the 1920s and 1930s were likely to convey unrepresentative class images. Most advertisers defined the market for their products as a relatively select audience of upper-class and upper-middle-class Americans. Even had they sought to depict the lives of these consumers with absolute fidelity, their ads would have mirrored only this select audience rather than society as a whole. . . .

One significant bias of advertisers deserves particular attention; and it is a bias that, paradoxically, offers us the prospect of using the advertisements of the 1920s and 1930s more confidently as a key to understanding certain realities of American culture. The ad creators of that era proudly proclaimed themselves missionaries of modernity. Constantly and unabashedly, they championed the new against the old, the modern against the old-fashioned. This bias, inherent in their economic function, ensured that advertisements would emphasize disproportionately those styles, classes, behaviors, and social circumstances that were new and changing. . . .

At the same time, advertisers came to recognize certain vacuums of advice in modern society. They had always offered advice in a narrow, prescriptive sense: use our product. Now they discovered a market for broader counsel and reassurance. In response, they gave advice that promoted the product while offering expertise and solace in the face of those modern complexities and impersonal judgments that made the individual feel incompetent and insecure. Advertisers, then as now, recognized a much larger stake in reflecting people's needs and anxieties than in depicting their actual circumstances and behavior. It was in their efforts to promote the mystique of modernity in styles and technology, while simultaneously assuaging the anxieties of consumers about losses of community and individual control, that they most closely mirrored historical reality—the reality of a cultural dilemma. . . .

Other professional elites—scientists, engineers, and industrial designers—also claimed to epitomize the dynamic forces of modernization, but adverstising agents insisted that they played a crucial role. Scientific inventions and technological advances fostered the expectation of change and the organization for continuous innovation that characterized modern society. But inventions and their technological applications made a dynamic impact only when the great mass of people learned of their benefits, integrated them into their lives, and came to lust for more new products. Modern technologies needed their heralds, advertising men contended. Modern styles and ways of life needed their missionaries. Advertising men were modernity's "town criers." They brought good news about progress. . . .

New industries were surging to the forefront in the 1920s. Nearly all of the glamor industries of the era—automobiles, radio, chemicals, movies, drugs, and electrical refrigeration—had established . . . a "face-to-face relationship" with the consuming public. Industrial giants like General Electric and Westinghouse, once primarily suppliers of equipment to other industries, increasingly sold products directly to individual consumers. The special modernity of advertising agents seemed exemplified by their strategic position on the interface of this dynamic new relationship between big business and its public. . . .

Advertisers thus celebrated the complexities and interdependencies of modern society, seeking to further rationalize the operations of the marketplace, to lubricate its mechanisms, and to achieve greater control over its functioning. With the maturing of industrialization, the consumer remained the most unpredictable and thus the most disruptive element in the economic system. If advertising agents could induce consumers to answer their needs by depending on more products offered them impersonally through the marketplace and could educate them to a predictable and enthusiastic demand for new products, then they would enhance the rationality and dynamism of the modern business system. . . .

The exhilaration created by the new pace of technological change and economic activity coexisted with deep anxieties about social disorder—anxieties symbolized by prohibition, immigration restrictions, and warnings of the dangers posed by the "new woman" and "flaming youth." Jazz, bobbed hair, cosmetics, the hip flask, and sexual frankness all flouted traditional moral standards and seemed to threaten family stability and paternal authority. The new media of movies and radio were nationalizing American culture, creating the specter of a country whose masses could be easily swayed by the latest fad.

Ad creators seized on the public's sense of an exciting yet disconcerting new tempo, reinforcing and amplifying this perception for their own purposes. They welcomed the economic forces that were propelling advertising toward an enhanced position of power and status in the society, and they explored strategies for transforming their clients' products into plausible solutions to the anxieties and dilemmas that arose from the pace of life and the scale of institutions in the new era. In the process, American advertising matured in style and content, gradually assuming what we now recognize as distinctly modern forms. . . .

Perhaps more than any other institution, American advertising adapted itself to the possibilities for exercising both a dynamic and a stabilizing influence during such an age. Advertising served preeminently as the spokesman for modernism. It exalted technological advances and disseminated the good news of progress to the millions. It promoted urban lifestyles and sought to educate consumers to master the new complexities of social interaction. But the very social and technological changes which advertising glorified also placed a burden of proof on those who wished to reassure an anxious public that society still operated on a comprehensible human scale—a scale within which people could expect their individual needs to be recognized and catered to. . . .

. . . Advertising, by linking itself with civilizing influences, could thus serve a redemptive function. It would not only improve the economic well-being of the consumer masses; it was destined to raise their cultural and intellectual standards as well. . . .

. . . Advertisements were *secular* sermons, exhortations to seek fulfillment through the consumption of material goods and mundane services. . . .

Any hope for uplift, for the missionary effect of the advertising writer, would have to come, if at all, not from the impact of the advertisements on the consumer's mind but from the new behavior and tastes that the ownership of products would induce. Since the products themselves would be the agents of uplift, advertisers could best carry out their mission as modernizers and civilizers by employing the most effective means—including frivolous entertainment . . . to put the products in the consumer's hands. In serving the cause of modernity, American advertising modernized its techniques. Ironically, it did so by responding to some of the most archaic qualities of a seemingly unsophisticated, emotional, intimacy-hungry public. . . .

. . . [R]eaders found themselves schooled in one of the most pervasive of all advertising tableaux of the 1920s—the parable of the Democracy of Goods. According to this parable, the wonders of modern mass production and distribution enabled every person to enjoy the society's most significant pleasure, convenience, or benefit. The definition of the particular benefit fluctuated, of course, with each client who employed the parable. But the cumulative effect of the constant reminders that "any woman can" and "every home can afford" was to publicize an image of American society in which concentrated wealth at the top of a hierarchy of social classes restricted no family's opportunity to acquire the most significant products. By implicitly defining "democracy" in terms of equal access to consumer products, and then by depicting the everyday functioning of that "democracy" with regard to one product at a time, these tableaux offered Americans an inviting vision of their society as one of incontestable equality.

In its most common advertising formula, the concept of the Democracy of Goods asserted that although the rich enjoyed a great variety of luxuries, the acquisition of their *one* most significant luxury would provide anyone with the ultimate in satisfaction. For instance, a Chase and Sanborn's Coffee tableau, with an elegant butler serving a family in a dining room with a sixteen-foot ceiling, reminded Chicago families that although "compared with the riches of the more fortunate, your way of life may seem modest indeed," yet no one—"king, prince, statesman, or capitalist"—could enjoy better coffee. . . .

The social message of the parable of the Democracy of Goods was clear. Antagonistic envy of the rich was unseemly; programs to redistribute wealth were unnecessary. The best things in life were already available to all at reasonable prices. . . .

. . . The Great Depression of the early 1930s, however, presented the American dream of individual success through equal access to ample opportunities with its most formidable challenge. Not only had advertising writers served as public spokesmen for a business system now brought under suspicion; they were now engaged, in their own agencies and corporate departments, in an increasingly desperate personal struggle for survival and success. . . .

. . . [C]opywriters recognized the centrality of the success creed to the dilemmas of depression-era Americans. But advertisers made no effort to learn popular attitudes in order to mirror

17

them. Rather, they invested themselves with a responsibility for moral leadership. By implicitly defining all other responses to the depression as cowardly, they sought to give a recommitment to hard work the force of a moral imperative. The appeal to courage did not invite a close examination of circumstances; rather it short-circuited any depression-inspired questions about the functioning and credibility of the American dream. . . .

. . . Depression advertising *looked* different. Of course, strategies for brand differentiation always insured that some advertisers would seek distinctive images by bucking style trends. But no one can glance through the advertisements of a 1932 issue of a popular magazine and mistake the prevalent style for that of a 1928 issue. Depression advertising was distinctively "loud," cluttered, undignified, and direct. . . .

Eventually these economic and occupational pressures were bound to affect the style and content of advertising copy. Advertisers did not like to become the bearers of bad news; still, they needed to make the messages about their products "newsworthy." To do so often meant to show how the product—in price, function, or symbolic value—was particularly necessary or attractive "in these times.". . .

. . . No single trend in advertising content characterized even the gravest years of the early 1930s. Even in 1933, most national advertisements offered no direct reflection of the existence of the depression. But gradually, more and more advertisers sought to empathize with, and perhaps to reflect, public concerns about econonomizing and job insecurity and popular yearnings for compensatory satisfactions. . . .

. . . [T]he parable of the Democracy of Goods gained even greater use as consolation. Psychologically, the depression could be overcome through compensatory satisfactions. Certain products, affordable by all, could provide pleasures no millionaire could surpass. "One joy you can afford," insisted Vigoro fertilizer, "is a Beautiful Garden." "Here—write like a millionaire!" beckoned the American Pencil Company. "A millionaire may ride in a sportier car, live in a richer home, and work at a bigger desk . . . but he can't write with a better pencil than *you* can. . . . And the price is ten cents, to everyone." Copywriters promoted easily affordable Edgeworth Pipe Tobacco not merely as a compensating pleasure but as a depression-inspired rediscovery of the truly satisfying. To the "thousands who had been swept away from the calmness and composure of pipe smoking by the speed of the Prosperity Era," Edgeworth offered an escape from "the tensions of work and business problems" and a return to "the solid things of life.". . .

The parable of the Democracy of Goods, including its dramatic depression versions, promised compensations for the lack of self-sufficiency and personal control inherent in the scale of a life lived among the multitudes. This parable offered consumers a sense of significant participation in the society, on an equality with the most privileged citizens, through specific and often trivial acts of consumption. In so doing, it brushed aside the question of whether average citizens could hope to retain the qualities of political participation and economic self-determination that they might have enjoyed in a society of smaller scale.

The Concerns of American Consumers

Many advertisers were convinced that American consumers were, quite literally, the "great unwashed." Their ads emphasized cultural values that society now considered to be of critical importance—appearance, cleanliness, pleasant odor, and fresh breath. As the prosperous years of the 1920s gave way to the Great Depression of the 1930s, ad writers increasingly emphasized these values, certain that they would make the difference in the continual struggle in this new era of unemployment and poverty. Excerpted from Juliann Sivulka, Soap, Sex, and Cigarettes: A Cultural History of American Advertising *(Belmont, CA, 1998), 158, 160, 162-63, 166-68, 199-201.*

What we know as mouthwash first sold as a "breath deodorant." Sales for the general antiseptic Listerine, invented by a St. Louis druggist named J. W. Lambert, moved slowly until Milton Feasley and Gordon Seagrove of the firm's Chicago ad agency, Williams & Cunnyngham, promoted the product as a remedy for bad breath. One simply did not talk about such personal matters

---

Excerpts reprinted from *Soap, Sex and Cigarettes: A Cultural History of American Advertising*, by Juliann Sivulka, 1998, Wadsworth Publishing Company.

in polite company, so the agency used the medical-sounding "halitosis" instead. Copywriter Milton Feasley created the halitosis idea in 1922. One expression of the concept became on[e] of the best-known advertising headlines: "Often a bridesmaid but never a bride." The headline continued with different copy and illustrations for three decades. For example, this classic 1925 ad created new anxieties:

> Edna's case was really a pathetic one. Like every woman, her primary ambition was to marry. Most of the girls of her set were married—or about to be. Yet not one possessed more grace or charm or loveliness than she. And as her birthdays crept gradually toward that tragic thirty-mark, marriage seemed farther from her life than ever. She was often a bridesmaid but never a bride.
>
> That's the insidious thing about halitosis (unpleasant breath). You, yourself, rarely know when you have it. And even your closest friends won't tell you.

But the friendly Listerine adviser could. Listerine worked as a "breath deodorant" and halted "food fermentation in the mouth and [left] the breath sweet, fresh, and clean."

Further installments of the dramatic Listerine campaign presented other social disasters, from missed invitations to ruined marriages, that supposedly could happen to anybody. One 1926 ad asked: "Was this a hint? This was the third time it had happened in a month: he the head of the concern, finding one of these advertisements on his desk, marked for his attention, no signature."

The campaign proved so successful that people's behavior changed. The morning mouthwash soon became as popular as the morning shower. To further boost sales, Listerine creatively introduced other uses for the product: a dandruff cure, an after-shave tonic, a cold and sore throat remedy, an astringent, and a deodorant; Listerine even developed its own brand of cigarettes. Annual ad expenditures for Listerine products rose from $100,000 in 1922 to $5 million in 1928, with Listerine generating a net $4 million profit over the same period.

With Listerine as a model, ad campaigns revolving around "advertising by fear" or "whisper copy" fostered new anxieties and contributed solutions every day. Yet all the ads carefully masked the "unmentionable" in sober, medical-sounding terms.

For example, Absorbine Jr. effectively treated the fungus "Tinea Trichophyton" (athlete's foot), Pompeiian massage cream eliminated "comedones" (blackheads), and Spencer corsets corrected "lordosis" (faulty posture).

Lever Brothers, the makers of Lifebuoy and Lux soap in Cambridge, Massachusetts, also were inspired by Listerine's ploy of creating a problem (halitosis) and then providing a solution. The company revised its advertising copy to reflect this stronger selling approach.

Since 1902 Lifebuoy had been advertised as "the soap that cleans and disinfects, purifies—at one operation." In 1928, however, a Lifebuoy soap ad assured consumers that the product would "protect" them from an even greater social disgrace: "B.O."—short for "Body Odor." Similarly, Lux originally had been promoted as a wonderful new product for "laundering fine fabrics"; and by the mid-1920s it could also preserve "soft, youthful, lovely feminine hands." In the early 1930s, however, Lever Brothers dramatically shifted gears and adopted a stronger sell. Lux could now prevent "undie odor": "She never omits her Daily Bath, yet wears underthings a SECOND DAY." As these stop-smelling pitches ran, business boomed for Lever Brothers.

Advertising the new product Kotex, made by Cellucotton Products Co. in Chicago, proved yet another delicate task. How did one mention the truly unmentionable? With the topic of menstruation a taboo, the early ads succeeded without using any descriptive words in the headline. A 1921 Kotex ad read: "Simplify the laundress problem," referring to the unwelcome chore of laundering soiled cloths or rags. "Kotex are good enough to form a habit, cheap enough to throw away, and easy to dispose of," explained the copy. In 1927 the Lord & Thomas agency claimed: "The Safe Solution of Women's Greatest Hygienic Problem, over 80 percent of the better class of women in America today employ Kotex" a product that "thoroughly deodorizes." Through friendly chatter the Kotex ads assured modern women of the value and convenience of the product while delicately avoiding an intimate discussion of feminine hygiene. Yet Kotex faced still another problem: women were too embarrassed to ask for the product by name. To address this issue, later Kotex ads included a new marketing device. Plain brown wrappers camouflaged the name Kotex on the packages; merchants displayed the product on the counter so a woman simply picked it up and left the money.

Once women did not have to ask for the product by name, sales rose. . . .

Selling the Cigarette Habit

The selling of cigarettes proved to be advertising's ultimate triumph of the decade. At that time many people considered cigarette smoking an undesirable habit. Moralists blasted cigarettes, referring to them as "coffin nails" and "gaspers." Henry Ford deemed cigarette smokers unemployable in a 1914 pamphlet. Others held that the cigarette smokers were most likely criminals, neurotics, or possibly drug addicts. The war and multimillion-dollar advertising campaigns changed all that. During and after World War I, cigarettes gained wider acceptance when both soldiers and civilians found smoking cigarettes to be more convenient, cheaper, and more sanitary than chewing tobacco.

To this audience R. J. Reynolds in Winston-Salem, North Carolina, directed its first nationally marketed cigarette, called Camel. The brand quickly achieved market dominance with an upscale-priced smoke that delivered a new tobacco taste. In no time George Washington Hill's American Tobacco Company in North Carolina created a richer, sweeter tobacco product, Lucky Strike cigarettes. The three major brands (Chesterfield was the third) then slugged it out for the market lead from 1917 until after World War II.

Hill hired hard-sell expert Albert J. Lasker of the Lord & Thomas agency and told him to do whatever was necessary to win the cigarette war. As a result, Lucky Strike advertising broke all previous records. Hill's enormous ad expenditures also brought the Lord & Thomas agency back into the ranks of the major agencies. In 1929 alone the American Tobacco Company accounted for over one-fourth of the agency's $40 million in billings. . . .

Hill, urged on by Lasker, jumped at the chance to reach an untapped audience—women—who would double the potential market. Until now advertising had supported the notion that the pleasures of smoking were for men only. But a number of women took up smoking during World War I as cigarette tobacco became milder and easier to use than the roll-your-own varieties (although the filter had not yet been invented). Still, society did not consider smoking an acceptable social practice for women.

Throughout the decade women smokers remained a controversial issue. For example, many colleges prohibited women from smoking on campus. Women also found themselves unable to smoke in railroad diners, in many smoking rooms in train stations, and on board ships. By the mid-1920s, however, some colleges had established smoking rooms, while streetcars, railroads, and shipping lines liberalized their regulations. Some railroads opened their smoking cars to women despite men's complaints that women occupied their seats; others installed separate smoking compartments for men and for women or allowed women to smoke in the dining car.

Advertising further fueled this cultural revolution. One 1912 ad for Velvet Tobacco showed a "respectable" woman sitting with a man who was smoking; "I wish I were a man," she mused, suggesting that she might like to smoke. Some ads hinted at this daring idea, while others took a more direct approach. In 1926 the Newell-Emmett agency daringly presented a poster showing a romantic moonlit seaside scene and a man lighting his Chesterfield with a woman perched beside him saying, "Blow some my way." These four words shocked many people. Yet Chesterfield resolutely carried on with its campaign, paving the way to the vast women's market. Hill and Lasker quickly sensed an opportunity for the Lucky Strike brand and pitched the female audience, appealing to women's growing sense of independence.

The Lucky Strike advertising campaign incorporated several major innovations. First, Hill was concerned that women were resisting the green packaging because it clashed with their clothes (the original pack had a red bull's-eye on a dark green background until 1942, when it changed to red on white). To solve the problem, he hired Edward L. Bernays, a public relations pioneer, who promoted the color green as fashionable in fashion shows so that the dark green Luckies packages would complement women's ensembles. Hill also used celebrities from the entertainment world, such [as] film stars, crooners, and jazz musicians, to promote his cigarettes. And for the first time women endorsed the product and popularized the image of the fashionable lady who, while she indeed smoked, still appeared stylish and respectable. Lucky Strike campaigns particularly favored testimonials from operatic sopranos, actresses, and society matrons, who attested to the positive effect Luckies had on their voices. One slogan ("Reach for a Lucky instead of a sweet") even drew protests from the candy industry. . . . Many marketers believe that this "sweet" campaign created more women smokers than any other single advertising effort. . . .

A "Hard Sell" for Hard Times

Advertising had helped spur the business boom in the 1920s, and some observers suggested that it could even prevent future economic downfalls. That is, advertising could best reverse the "depression state of mind" by hammering out messages of reassurance. But advertising had failed to stem the onset of the Depression, and agencies soon felt the tremors of the stock market crash. . . .

Economic and professional concerns eventually affected the look and content of advertising in the early 1930s. Cost-conscious advertisers used color and illustrations sparingly, substituting extensive text in a multitude of typefaces to grab attention. Louder headlines, strident hard-sell copy, and gross exaggerations appeared as pseudoscientific arguments and appeals to emotion. Ads especially capitalized on consumers' intensified economic and personal insecurities. . . .

Advertisers worked hard to show how their client's product was necessary or attractive in terms of price, function, or value. They also sought to empathize with the Depression-wracked public's concerns about economizing and employment. In the process admakers found two appeals of immense value. One obvious tactic was a blatant emphasis on price. Although hardly a new idea, these economy appeals intensified in the early 1930s, as evidenced by the emergence of supermarkets and ads featuring price as the attention-getting element. The other tactic tapped into consumers' economic insecurities. . . .

A heavy emphasis on dollar figures gave some national advertisements the look of retail ads. Some automobile ads even employed the traditional bargain-offer format that featured a crossed-out price. Other ads emphasized the potential savings associated with purchasing a given product. For instance, an ad for Hoover vacuum cleaners boasted: "The richest woman in the world can have no finer electric cleaner than any woman can have and for as little as $4.50 down." A Fabray window shade ad argued that people should not throw away filthy window coverings, but instead should wash them: "Now, Window Shades That

Are Really Washable . . . Yet Cost Only 45 Cents." Listerine toothpaste ads suggested another method to cope with tough times: "See what you can buy with the $3 you save" (that is, the money one saved after a year of buying a Listerine product at 25 cents a tube rather than other brands at 50 cents). Listerine ads listed potential uses of the money—purchases ranging from galoshes and underwear to milk and other staples. The economic appeal also addressed the mushrooming demand for "something for nothing," as contests, premiums, prizes, and two-for-one promotions appeared everywhere.

At the same time, advertisers' attempts to sell more products reflected their growing desperation. Traditional slice-of-life stories tapped emotions such as guilt, fear, shame, and blame to reinforce advertising appeals. These ads conveyed a common message: "If you don't buy this product, you'll be sorry."

Unease Over the Effects of Advertising

Michael Schudson tends to be critical of advertising's influence over American society. Still, he claims that advertisers have been unable to cause profound changes in social values. In this passage, he discusses the relationship between cigarette advertising and the increase in smoking among women during the 1920s. Excerpted from Advertising, the Uneasy Persuasion: Its Dubious Impact on American Society *(New York, 1984), 43, 179-80, 183, 192, 197, 207, 235-37.*

Here I speak only of advertising's specific power to sell specific goods, and that power is clearly limited. . . .

. . . I will develop this point through a case study of the growing popularity of the cigarette in the 1920s and, in doing so, will make a second point: that major consumer changes are rarely wrought by advertising. Advertising followed rather than led the spread of cigarette usage and it was the convenience and democracy of the cigarette, coupled with specific, new opportunities for its use, that brought the cigarette into American life. . . .

The spread of cigarette smoking, particularly among women, was one of the most visible signs of change in consumption practices in the 1920s, and one that has been cited frequently as evidence of the new powers of advertising and marketing. Between 1918 and 1940, American consumption grew from 1.70 to 5.16 pounds of cigarette tobacco per adult. During the same period, advertising budgets of the tobacco companies bulged, movies pictured elegant men and women smoking, and public relations stunts promoted cigarettes.

Some contemporary observers concluded that advertising *caused* the increase in cigarette smoking among women. For instance, in 1930, Clarence True Wilson, board secretary of the Methodist Episcopal Church, declared: "If the advertising directed to women ceased, it is probable that within five years the smoking woman would be the rare exception." Scholars in recent years have accepted a similar view. Erik Barnouw, for instance, holds that advertising was responsible for bringing women into the cigarette market.

This conclusion is difficult to sustain for a number of reasons, the most obvious of which is that tens of thousands of women began smoking cigarettes in the 1920s *before* a single advertisement was directed toward them. It is more accurate to observe that cigarette smoking among women led tobacco companies to advertise toward the female market than to suggest that advertising created the market in the first place. The mass media played a role in spreading the cigarette habit among women, but it was primarily the information conveyed in news stories, not the persuasion attempted in advertisements, that helped in the first instance to legitimate smoking among women in the 1920s. . . .

Meanwhile, cigarette manufacturers were cautious in appealing directly to women. Curtis Wessel, editor of the *United States Tobacco Journal*, wrote in 1924 that "all responsible tobacco opinion" found the habit of women smoking so "novel" that "it would not be in good taste for tobacco men as parties in interest to stir a particle toward or against a condition with whose beginnings they had nothing to do and whose end, if any, no one can foresee."

When advertisers did begin to address women directly, they did so cautiously. The first notable cigarette ad directed toward women was a Chesterfield ad in 1926 showing a romantic couple at night, the man smoking, the woman sitting next to him, with the caption, "Blow Some My Way." Most ads for cigarettes, even ads with an audience of women in mind, showed only men smoking. The *New Yorker* in 1926 printed a full page ad for Miltiades Egyptian cigarettes that featured a drawing captioned, "After Theatre," with a man and a woman in evening dress. The man is smoking and says to the woman, "Somehow or other Shakespeare's heroines seem more feminine in modern garb and smoking cigarettes. . . . " He advises her to exercise care in choosing a cigarette—but she, as usual, is not shown smoking. A Camel cigarette ad in *Time* in 1926 shows two men lighting up, two women looking on. An ad in *Time* for Fatima Turkish Cigarettes claims, "It's What the Younger Crowd Thinks About It!" and shows a man and a woman waterskiing, but only the man smoking. A Camel cigarette ad in *The Outlook* in 1927 shows two men and a woman at a nightclub, both men smoking and the woman not smoking. . . .

. . . The cigarette was . . . a focus of anxiety and antagonism toward the "new woman" and the changing sex roles she embodied. Cigarette advertising provided a way to legitimate and naturalize women's smoking. It was a weapon in the fight among tobacco companies for market share, of course, but it was, like most advertising, conservative, venturing to challenge established ways in the population only when evidence of new market patterns was in plain view. Despite the importance of the commercial interests involved in spreading the use of cigarettes among women, the change that occurred was a cultural one. It was made possible by changes in the cigarette product itself, by World War I's transformation of social habits, and by a new class of women who sponsored the cigarette in its political and social battles. In the 1920s, a cigarette in the hands of a woman meant a change in the language of social interaction. Such changes may be vigorously contested. They were at that time, just as they have been more recently when "Ms" and "he or she" entered the spoken language and came to be used, at least in some circles, naturally. That advertising has played a role since the late 1920s in promoting smoking among women should not blind us to the fact that this change in consumption patterns, like many others, has roots deep in cultural change and political conflict that advertising often responds to but rarely creates. . . .

This cigarette case study has tried to reach a little deeper, to recognize the social roots of significant changes in consumption patterns and to characterize what a change in consumer activity might signify. It also has served as a reminder that advertising generally works to reinforce consumer trends rather than to initiate them. Critics of advertising in the 1920s and today have regarded the adoption of cigarette smoking by women as a clear-cut proof of the power of persuasive advertising to dramatically change consumer habits. It is not so; the matter turns out to be not so obvious at all. . . .

. . . Perhaps, [the defenders of advertising and marketing] admit, there are things wrong with a consumer culture, but advertising is not responsible for them. Marketing, they say, merely identifies and responds to human needs and does not—cannot—create the motivations that propel the race of consumption. They are appalled that critics imagine they have such overwhelming powers. They easily brush off criticism that attributes to advertising untold magical influence, extraordinary psychological sophistication, or primary responsibility for creating a consumer culture. They show that they work to reach people already predisposed to the product they are selling, that their appeals stress solid product information as often as they engage in emotional manipulation, and that the consumer is so fickle and the world so complex that their best-laid plans go astray as often as not.

All of this is true. But it is a much less sturdy defense of marketing than it appears. . . .

First, marketers do not actually seek to discover what consumers "want" but what consumers want *from among commercially viable choices*. . . . Marketers keep the consumer in mind only to the degree that the consumer defines his or her own prospects in terms agreeable to marketers. Thus consumers are not asked if they would prefer public television to advertising-supported television or public transportation to private automobiles or government-supported health care to private physicians.

Developers survey consumers to find out what kind of housing project they prefer, but they do not ask if a public park would be more desirable. . . .

. . . In short, the consumers the marketers listen to are not persons, not citizens, but thin voices choosing from among a set of predetermined options. The "people" the marketers are concerned with are only those people or those parts of people that fit into the image of the consumer the marketer has created.

Second, marketers do not listen to all people equally. There is nothing democratic or populist about an approach that listens ten times as carefully to the person with $10,000 in discretionary income as to the person with $1,000. But that is what marketers do. The point is to make money, not to please people. The marketers keep their eyes on the main prize—pocketbooks, not persons. This yields an array of consumer choices top heavy in luxury, and it sometimes works directly to diminish the array of goods available to the person of modest means. For instance, in the competition for the affluent person's dollar, more and more extras become standard equipment on automobiles and other products, and the low-income consumer has no choice but to go deeper into debt to pay for the simplest model, now weighted with superfluous "standard" equipment. In Third World countries, national and multinational corporations provide a highly inappropriate array of products for local needs because they serve largely the very small affluent population in those nations. This is especially no-ticeable and dangerous in an area like that of health care: "Since middle-income and rich consumers represent the main market for modern drugs, pharmaceutical companies concentrate on fur-nishing remedies for middle-class ailments like general fatigue, headaches, and constipation rather than for low-income diseases like leprosy, filariasis, and tuberculosis."

Third, marketers wrongly assume that since "good advertis-ing kills a bad product," they can do little harm; people will only buy what they find satisfying. This works, as I have argued, only if people have enough information available to know what the range of possibilities is and how to purchase wisely. This is not true for many populations: poor people, children, Third World peoples, people entering new social roles, people with limited time or uncertain emotional stability for making decisions. Even with educated, middle-class adults, where the product sold is complex and where the normal adult is not able to make informed comparisons among products, advertising or other marketing practices can lead people to buy things that they do not need, things that will not "satisfy" their desires, and things that are not good for them.

Questions

1. *How does the advertising and marketing process work? If you were an advertising executive, how would you introduce a new product to the buying public?*
2. *According to advertising executives, what kinds of problems bothered Americans during the 1920s? Did their concerns remain the same, or did new problems emerge during the 1930s? How did advertisers attempt to "solve" these problems?*
3. *Were advertisers simply trying to earn a paycheck by selling more products, or did they have more altruistic motives? Did advertisers feel that Americans would be better off if they consumed more products and, if so, why and how?*
4. *Compare and contrast how Sivluka and Schudson treat cigarette advertising to women. Why did cigarette consumption among women grow so dramatically during the 1920s? Were advertisers responsible for this change, or were other factors involved?*

Words and Images:
Ads and Advertisers
During the 1920s and 1930s

Although advertising executives spent much of their time publicizing products, many also publicized themselves and their profession. Since many Americans initially regarded advertising as little better than fraud, it is hardly surprising that ad writers attempted to convince the American people that advertising was a legitimate profession. Sometimes they went well beyond that, often claiming that advertising was central to social harmony and continued economic prosperity in the United States. Only advertisers, they said, could adequately direct the enormous flows of manufactured consumer goods from the factories to the consumer; only advertisers could predict and regulate the buying patterns of American consumers.

The best evidence of the advertisers' craft lies in ads themselves. These ads primarily appeared on the new medium of the radio and in national circulation magazines. Radio ads lose much of their appeal when transcribed into text, but print ads remain quite persuasive. For many advertisers, these ads were not just sales pitches; they were works of art, and a testimony to the skills of advertising copywriters and illustrators. Many of those involved in the advertising industry thought of themselves as artists and, like artists, they tapped into a deep well of human emotions—desire, love, happiness, fear, and insecurity. Many of those themes, so readily identifiable in ads from the 1920s and 1930s, still appear in today's far more technically sophisticated advertisements, although often more subtly. One thing has changed, though. Ads in the 1920s and 1930s did not target impressionable children and adolescents to nearly the same extent as they do today.

An Advertising Executive in Action

While many advertising executives wrote accounts of their professional and personal lives, these tend to be rather shallow and one-dimensional. One of the best first-person descriptions of the day-to-day activities of an ad executive comes from Fairfax M. Cone, With All Its Faults: A Candid Account of Forty Years in Advertising *(Boston, 1969), 90-92, 94-97.*

The half-dozen Roos Bros. stores, in San Francisco and the San Francisco Bay area . . . were characterized even then by a policy of innovation that approached audacity. The Roos stores were the first in the country to advertise "wardrobes" rather than "suits" for men. These were based on the combinations that were possible with matching coat and trousers and complementary and contrasting sports jackets and slacks. Just so, Roos Bros. discovered a gold mine that unlike most of the diggings in California has been an unfailing producer every year since.

Colonel Robert Roos was a brilliant, irascible potentate who moodily ran his satrapy from a black-walled, white-carpeted throne room whose doors were electrically opened and closed, and at whose bar the very simplest agreements were generally sealed only after long and often tempestuous arguments, but in rare old scotch or bourbon.

I very nearly was not invited to sample either one.

It was strictly a hunch on the part of the Colonel's advertising manager that brought me to the inner sanctum at all. The hunch belonged to an extraordinary woman. Her name is Eleanor Lyons. She never, to my knowledge, has had an advertising idea that wasn't practical and worthwhile, because that is the way her mind works. You could almost watch it under her nicely coiffed, prematurely gray hair. She knew precisely what she wanted and she outlined it in broad terms. Then she let you work out the details.

What she wanted from us was advertising that would give the Roos stores some of the aura of authority that Kenneth Collins had built into the advertising for Macy's in New York.

"There must be something better, something more important, than merely another retail clothier shouting low prices," Eleanor Lyons insisted. "There must be a way to establish an important character, a unique personality, to be an institution, like Macy's. Or, if you won't laugh, like Tiffany."

I said I thought there was. And I told Eleanor Lyons that I thought I knew how to do this.

But when I was let into the Colonel's black office, through the electric doors, I wasn't so sure that I wasn't out of my depth. Wanting not to seem cocky (which I certainly didn't feel) I ventured the opinion that Roos Bros. was doing a mighty good advertising job as things stood.

"You couldn't be more right," the Colonel boomed. "One hundred thousand dollars a month right. Twelve hundred thousand dollars a year right. It is a crazy idea of this dear girl that some advertising agency can do something for us that we ourselves can't do much better. Tell me what it is that we should expect from some advertising agency that has never sold a necktie or a suit."

"Nothing," the Colonel said, answering his own question. "Nothing. Absolutely nothing."

The answer in the man's mind appeared to be clear; as far as he was concerned the matter was settled. But the distaste with which the Colonel had spit out the words "advertising agency," and on "some" advertising agency that was obviously Lord & Thomas, made it necessary for me to make him eat those words if I could.

By trying to be polite, I had let Eleanor Lyons down badly. I hadn't been adroit enough to follow the lead she had given me, and the Colonel had pounced on my pleasantry and turned it against both of us. He was a hard man to sell, and I hadn't helped his lady at all.

It was midday on a Friday when Colonel Roos coldly pressed a button in a panel on his desk and opened the way out of his office. I wished that I might never have to see him again; but Eleanor Lyons had told me that the man knew Albert Lasker very well, and I knew that I would have to make another try, disagreeable as this might be.

On Monday I telephoned him to say that I wanted to see him.

"I want to show you a newspaper advertisement," I said. "It will show you how to do everything Eleanor Lyons was trying to tell you and all she wants to do in advertising, and it will do everything you're already doing well better than you've ever done it."

I didn't sound like me even to myself. But the Colonel's unwillingness to listen to me after my soft opening three days before had made me furious. Also, there was the possible involvement of Albert Lasker in the affair. I was a new, insecure young manager, and I couldn't have his friend casting doubts about me.

"All right," the Colonel said, with what seemed a great effort. "I'll see what you've got, but I haven't much time." And off I started with my exhibits.

The idea that had come to me in Eleanor Lyons's office had grown on me on Friday night, in bed, which is where I have always done my best work, particularly under pressure, and most particularly when angry. I had written the full-page newspaper advertisement on Saturday, and had it laid out and illustrated on Sunday by a puzzled young art director named Harry Fletcher who couldn't understand why he should give up a picnic with his girl for a cranky non-client.

In the beginning, I was only working to square myself with Eleanor Lyons and to build up my case if I had to use it for Albert Lasker; but by the time I got the Colonel on the telephone on Monday morning I had no doubt that I would accomplish both my objectives at Colonel Roos's expense. What I planned to do was show the man the advertisement I had made, get his acknowledgment that the idea was good for a long series, then make him an elaborate gift of it and depart on my high horse.

When I showed him the advertisement he stared at it for several minutes, saying nothing. Then he got up from behind his enormous black desk and standing between the two silk flags that flanked it at the rear, the stars and stripes of the United States and the flag of his own California National Guard regiment, the Colonel cleared his throat and said, with full military dignity, "I knew you would come through."

I had hoped to win the day. But I only tied it. Colonel Roos had known very well that I would react to his taunts; for despite his dislike of agencies (and their fees, in this case) he wanted Eleanor Lyons to have her way.

The advertisement, which was framed at top and bottom with an institutional promise from Roos Bros., and which told the story of the featured merchandise in specific terms of design and manufacture instead of the generalities and tired expletives that were the rule in retail men's clothing advertising, became the pattern for a series that ran unchanged in format for almost ten years. . . .

Our second venture into the retail field, triggered by our success with Roos Bros., proved to be more educational than lucrative. This was with the Safeway stores which, traditionally, had run large newspaper advertisements that were really no more than price listings (the private label product accounts being handled independently and apart from the shopper pages).

The shopper advertisements were almost repulsively ugly, and a little research indicated to us that most housewives paid a minimum of attention to the listings except to scan the lines of heavy black type for real bargains. Where there were no deeply cut prices the advertisements, even in full facing pages, apparently had no tangible effect. They merely kept the stores' name before the public.

No one who was a passionate follower of Albert Lasker could believe that this was truly advertising. Or that the prodigious space that was involved couldn't be made more productive.

Again we set to work, as we had with the sterile Roos Bros. advertisements, to transform the Safeway newspaper pages into something that rewarded readers for their attention. By designing the pages in orderly columns and reducing the extra bold type, we made space for menu suggestions, recipes, party hints, even diets; and facts about Safeway's procurement of all the items of fresh produce, meat and dairy products that were available at Safeway stores on an exclusive basis.

It didn't matter, we reasoned, where one bought Wheaties or Bisquick or Carnation milk or Jell-O; wherever these well-known products were purchased they were the same. Moreover, Safeway's private labels and usually lower prices on similar packaged groceries had a long way to go to prove superiority. On the other hand, it was possible to show persuasive and memorable reasons why meat and produce at Safeway were fresher and more select because of Safeway's tremendous buying ability and its massive private transportation system that hurried food to market. We reasoned that if we attracted customers for these good reasons, they would buy the nonexclusive groceries at the same time.

We asked people to take note of the Safeway trucks they passed on the highways at night, bringing huge quantities of fresh fruit and vegetables and meat and milk to market. And we mentioned the courtesy of the road that the drivers of those trucks exhibited.

What we undertook was a kind of public relations advertising. We tried to make friends by being friendly, rather than by continuously assaulting the newspaper readers with fat black type in a cascade of prices that tumbled together dry groceries, laundry products, candy, disinfectants, small hardware, shoe polish, cheese, etc., in an inebriate jumble.

But if the Safeway management thought well of our efforts, the store managers had very different ideas. Years later, as a director of Montgomery Ward & Company, I encountered the same lack of interest in public relations advertising. The conclusion I drew was that most store managers are like most salesmen. They are usually so price-conscious, so demoralized by lower price competition whenever it raises its little pointed head, so demanding of a price advantage that they think of little else. . . .

Our noble experiment with Roos Bros. was a notable failure at Safeway. There was no Eleanor Lyons who was dissatisfied with the advertising situation the way she had been, there was no Colonel Roos to back her up, however testily. Not until a dozen years later, when Franklin J. Lunding and George Clements of the Jewel Tea Company initiated similar advertising in Chicago was the idea vindicated. Fresh, informative advertising gave the Jewel stores an inviting character that was followed up by alert, carefully trained managers and department heads, and Jewel became the dominant food distributor in the area. . . .

Advertising as a Religion

Bruce Barton was a partner in several New York City advertising agencies. While he was perhaps one of the best known advertisers in the United States, he was not highly regarded within the advertising profession. Instead, his fame comes from a most unusual book, in which he asserts that advertising agencies—and advertising executives—are entitled to positions of special influence in American society. The Man Nobody Knows: A Discovery of the Real Jesus *(Indianapolis, 1925),* 23, 27, 92, 104, 107, 143, 124-26, 129-30, 138-40, 146-47, 149, 153, 162-63, 177.

He [Jesus] picked up twelve men from the bottom ranks of business and forged them into an organization that conquered the world.

When the man had finished his reading he exclaimed, "This is a man nobody knows."

"Some day," said he, "some one will write a book about Jesus. Every business man will read it and send it to his partners and his salesmen. For it will tell the story of the founder of modern business." . . .

Nowhere is there such a startling example of executive success as the way in which that organization [of the twelve disciples] was brought together. . . .

Having gathered together his organization, there remained for Jesus the tremendous task of training it. . . .

. . . Assuredly there was no demand for a new religion; the world was already over-supplied. And Jesus proposed to send forth eleven men and expect them to substitute his thinking for all existing religious thought! . . .

Surely no one will consider us lacking in reverence if we say that every one of the "principles of modern salesmanship" on which business men so much pride themselves, are brilliantly exemplified in Jesus' talk and work. . . .

It would be easy to multiply examples, taking each of his parables and pointing out the keen knowledge of human motives on which it is based. In a later chapter we shall have something more to say of these parables—the most powerful advertisements of all time. . . .

. . . The parable of the Good Samaritan is the greatest advertisement of all time. . . .

I am not a doctor, or lawyer or critic but an advertising man. As a profession advertising is young; as a force it is as old as the

---

Excerpts reprinted from *The Man Nobody Knows: A Discovery of the Real Jesus,* by Bruce Barton, 1924, Grosset & Dunlap Publishers.

world. The first four words ever uttered, "Let there be light," constitute its charter. . . .

. . . In the first place he [Jesus] recognized the basic principle that all good advertising is news. . . .

Can you imagine the next day's issue of the *Capernaum News*, if there had been one?

PALSIED MAN HEALED
JESUS OF NAZARETH CLAIMS RIGHT TO
FORGIVE SINS

PROMINENT SCRIBES OBJECT
"BLASPHEMOUS," SAYS LEADING CITIZEN.
"BUT ANYWAY I CAN WALK," HEALED MAN
RETORTS

[another example]

PROMINENT TAX COLLECTOR JOINS
NAZARETH FORCES

MATTHEW ABANDONS BUSINESS TO PROMOTE
NEW CULT
* * *
GIVES LARGE LUNCHEON . . .

These are Jesus' works, done in Jesus' name. If he were to live again, in these modern days, he would find a way to make them known—to be advertised by his service, not merely by his sermons. One thing is certain: he would not neglect the market-place. Few of his sermons were delivered in synagogues. . . .

No; the present day market-place is the newspaper and the magazine. Printed columns are the modern thoroughfares; published advertisements are the cross-roads where the sellers and the buyers meet. Any issue of a national magazine is a world's fair, a bazaar filled with the products of the world's work. . . . That every other voice should be raised in such great market-places, and the voice of Jesus of Nazareth be still—this is a vital omission which he would find a way to correct. He would be a national advertiser today, I am sure, as he was the great advertiser of his own day. . . .

. . . Every advertising man ought to study the parables of Jesus in the same fashion, schooling himself in their language. . . .

. . . How often you must read and read before you discover just what it is that the advertiser wants you to do. Jesus had no introductions. . . .

. . . A sixty-eight word prayer, he said, contained all that men needed to say or God to hear. What would be his verdict on most of our prayers and our speeches and our advertisements? . . .

Much brass has been sounded and many cymbals tinkled in the name of advertising; but the advertisements which persuade people to act are written by men who have an abiding respect for the intelligence of their readers, and a deep sincerity regarding the merits of the goods they have to sell. . . .

But what interests us most in . . . [the] one recorded incident of his boyhood is the fact that for the first time he defined the purpose of his career. He did not say, "Wist ye not that I must practise preaching?" or "Wist ye not that I must get ready to meet the arguments of men like these?" The language was quite different, and well worth remembering. "Wist ye not that I must be about my father's *business*?" he said. He thought of his life as *business*. What did he mean by business? To what extent are the principles by which he conducted his business applicable to ours? And if he were among us again, in our highly competitive world, would his business philosophy work? . . .

So we have the main points of his business philosophy:

1. Whoever will be great must render great service.
2. Whoever will find himself at the top must be willing to lose himself at the bottom.
3. The big rewards come to those who travel the second, undemanded mile.

The GREATEST MOTHER in the WORLD

 Stretching forth her hands to all in need; to Jew or Gentile, black or white; knowing no favorite, yet favoring all.

Ready and eager to comfort at a time when comfort is most needed. Helping the little home that's crushed beneath an iron hand by showing mercy in a healthy, human way; rebuilding it, in fact, with stone on stone; replenishing empty bins and empty cupboards; bringing warmth to hearts and hearths too long neglected.

Seeing all things with a mother's sixth sense that's blind to jealousy and meanness; seeing men in their true light, as naughty children — snatching, biting, bitter—but with a hidden side that's quickest touched by mercy.

Reaching out her hands across the sea to No Man's land; to cheer with warmer comforts thousands who must stand and wait in stenched and crawling holes and water-soaked entrenchments where cold and wet bite deeper, so they write, than Boche steel or lead.

She's warming thousands, feeding thousands, healing thousands from her store; the Greatest Mother in the World—the RED CROSS.

Every Dollar of a Red Cross War Fund goes to War Relief

World War I redeemed the image of advertising in America. Federal government agencies and charities like the Red Cross employed ad agencies to create national advertising campaigns that effectively persuaded Americans to give money, save food, join the military, or, more ominously, to hate everything German.

LYDIA E. PINKHAM'S
VEGETABLE COMPOUND.

A Sure Cure for all FEMALE WEAK-
NESSES, Including Leucorrhœa, Ir-
regular and Painful Menstruation,
Inflammation and Ulceration of
the Womb, Flooding, PRO-
LAPSUS UTERI, &c.

By the late 1800s, the most visually enticing ads extolled the virtues of patent medicines—"cure-alls" that really cured almost nothing, and were often harmful and occasionally lethal. These ads tainted the image of advertising in general, and consumers often equated advertising with fraud.

Nineteenth-century advertisements were primarily descriptive in nature. Instead of creating demand for a product, they merely informed buyers that certain items were available for purchase. There was little expectation that ads would actually help to create demand for a product.

One of the hallmarks of modern advertising is that it promises a vast array of intangible benefits—love, happiness, excitement—if the consumer will only buy the product. This ad, for the Borden Company, explicitly guarantees "happiness" and also offers romance, marriage, and sex—a considerable list of benefits from a can of sweetened condensed milk, to say the least. Also notice how ads from the 1920s used far more text, and correspondingly smaller visuals, than modern ads, and how they reinforced existing social values (a woman must be a good cook in order to land a husband).

During the 1920s "Chain stores" like Piggly Wiggly (we would call them "supermarkets" today) radically changed shopping patterns. Shoppers, accustomed to the limited choices of corner stores and street vendors, had to be taught how to read labels and then choose products from the shelf, rather than ask a grocer to assemble their order. Many shoppers found this new way of shopping almost incomprehensible—one chain store owner found that no one would use his new shopping carts until he paid "fake" shoppers to push carts around the store, thus showing the actual customers how to manage this unfamiliar technology. Ads also eased the public's anxiety about these new stores.

"Yeast builds resistance,"

says PROF. DOCTOR PAUL REYHER

famous lecturer at the University of Berlin

"THE MEDICINAL USES *of yeast are many-sided. There is a high percentage of Vitamin B in yeast... Vitamin B bears a very close relation to the proper functioning of the nervous system. It also improves the appetite, regulates metabolism, promotes growth and raises the body's power of resistance to every kind of infection... One can see, therefore, that yeast contains a remarkable healing factor.*"

ANOTHER of the great medical leaders of Europe to add his voice to the movement of health preparedness is Prof. Dr. Paul Reyher, of the University of Berlin.

Dr. Reyher has made an exhaustive study of yeast. His findings extend new hope to all who suffer from indigestion, headaches, nervousness, depression, too frequent colds and sore throat—sure signs of constipation and lowered vitality.

In a recent survey throughout the United States, half the doctors reporting said they prescribed fresh yeast for constipation and its attendant ills.

Fleischmann's Yeast is fresh. Unlike dried or killed yeast it contains millions of living, active yeast plants. As these live yeast plants pass daily through your system, they rouse the muscles that control elimination, combat harmful poisons. Your digestion improves. Your skin clears.

Eat three cakes of Fleischmann's Yeast every day, one cake before each meal or between meals, plain or in water (hot or cold). To get full benefit from yeast you must eat it regularly and over a sufficient period of time. At all grocers and many leading cafeterias, lunch counters and soda fountains. Buy two or three days' supply at a time, as it will keep in a cool, dry place. Start now!

Write for latest booklet on Yeast in the diet—free. Health Research Dept. C-123, The Fleischmann Company, 701 Washington St., New York, N.Y.

FROM THROAT TO COLON is one continuous tube. 90% of ills start here. Poisons from clogged intestines easily spread through the system, lowering resistance to disease. But here is where yeast works. "Yeast builds resistance," says Dr. Reyher. It keeps the entire intestinal tract clean, active and healthy. Eat Fleischmann's Yeast regularly.

PROF. DR. PAUL REYHER

Lecturer, University of Berlin, on Vitamins, X-Ray and Pediatrics; Director, Children's Hospital, Berlin, which he built and equipped. The Germans refer to this hospital as "the jewel box" because of its perfect appointments and beauty of structure.

UNIVERSITY OF BERLIN, where Dr. Reyher is a noted lecturer.

FLEISCHMANN'S YEAST
for HEALTH

In a decade when many Americans increasingly believed that the values of science and "modernity" were becoming more important than those of religion, advertisers attempted to depict their products as both modern and scientific. Although the Fleischmann Company, manufacturers of brewers' yeast, suffered during the early years of Prohibition, an ad campaign stressing the scientific and health values of yeast saved the company and made Fleischmann's Yeast a household name.

45

Ad writers consulted a medical dictionary and discovered the word "halitosis." This ominous-sounding word meant nothing worse than bad breath, but Listerine ads suggested that this "flaw" would consign women to a lifetime of spinsterhood.

He had to fight himself so hard...
he didn't put it over

YES, he was his own worst enemy. His appearance was against him and he knew it. Oh why had he neglected the bath that morning, the shave, the change of linen! Under the other fellow's gaze it was hard to forget that cheap feeling. There's self-respect in soap and water. The clean-cut chap can look any man in the face and tell him the facts—for when you're clean, your appearance fights *for* you.

There's self-respect in SOAP & WATER

PUBLISHED BY THE ASSOCIATION OF AMERICAN SOAP AND GLYCERINE PRODUCERS, INC., TO AID THE WORK OF CLEANLINESS INSTITUTE

Many advertisers sincerely believed that they had a mission to teach ordinary Americans how they could improve their lives through consumption. At a time when many Americans bathed no more than once a week, the looming "conscience" figure in this ad reminds the consumer that daily bathing with soap and water will lead to success at the workplace. Advertisers sought to uplift less-fortunate Americans who, in this case, quite literally constituted the "great unwashed masses."

The emerging value system of the 1920s placed less emphasis on "old" values like honor, duty, morality, and character, and greater emphasis on "new" values of individualism, achievement, personality, and appearance. The Camay ad says nothing about the character of the woman at the left of the picture, but says everything about her appearance. This she owes to Camay—"the soap of beautiful women"—which promises not only radiant skin but also the intangible benefits of excitement, romance, and sex. The scowling women to the right will never enjoy these benefits, because they use some other soap—can we assume, by extension, that all other soaps must be "the soap of ugly women?"

The man on the sofa may be a millionaire, or a Nobel laureate, or even the president of the United States. But he will never prevail in affairs of the heart because he has committed the unforgivable sin of wearing ungartered socks (in an age before elastic, men used calf garters to hold up their socks). Once again, the ad's emphasis is on the readily identifiable external values of image and appearance, not the older internal values of character and honor.

"She looks old enough to be his mother"

"Read this little book *carefully*, dear. . . . It explains things so much better than I can"

These ads for Lysol blend the 1920s interest in appearance with the desire of ad writers to be advisers and confidants for the supposedly uneducated American buying public. Both ads offer a free booklet "The Scientific Side of Health and Youth" (note the emphasis on science and on the intangible value of youth) that both pushed Lysol and helped the company track the readership of its print ads in various publications. In "Read this little book carefully," a mother is admitting that a distant and faceless corporation is better equipped than she to give her daughter advice on "feminine hygiene." It should be pointed out that, during the 1920s, one of the typical, if unacknowledged, uses of Lysol was as a post-coital spermicidal douche.

The 1926 Chesterfield "Blow some my way" ad marked a milestone in advertisers" efforts to gradually erode social taboos against women smoking in public. While the woman is not so radical as to light her own cigarette, she is receptive to the idea of inhaling her mate's second-hand smoke. Foreign women, like the Russian actress Nazimova, were often perceived as being more exotic than American women, and less subject to social taboos against smoking. Again, the advertisers' intent was to gradually render female smoking acceptable to mainstream Americans. By the end of the 1920s women openly reached for Lucky Strikes and other brands, though whether advertising caused this behavioral shift or was instead a product of it remains open to debate.

Few concepts better illustrate the social consciousness of ad writers than the idea of the democracy of goods. Many ad writers were genuinely troubled by the seemingly inescapable tendency of capitalism to create wide disparities in income and wealth (which worked against the cherished notion of "all men are created equal.") Some reasoned that they could help to create a democracy of goods—a society in which all Americans would be equal because they consumed the same products, or goods. The working-class man in the center (note his characteristic cap) does not feel resentment toward the unseen owner of the luxury car, and he certainly does not exhibit any desire to overthrow the capitalist system in favor of socialism or communism—each of which were very real alternatives in industrialized countries at that time—merely because both social classes have access to the same tires.

As the surface prosperity of the "Roaring Twenties" gave way to the hardships of the Great Depression, most Americans placed more emphasis on saving money rather than on acquiring the latest and greatest products. This Listerine toothpaste ad lists a price—almost unthinkable during the 1920s—and shows how thrift consumers can save enough money to buy important items for their families.

With fully a quarter of the American workforce unemployed during the depression, ad writers prayed on parents' fears that their children would fail in life, unless . . . Union Central life insurance could prevent an adolescent from being one of the forty-two out of forty-three children who failed in life, and caffeine-free Postum would save a child from the humiliation of being the class dunce.

Questions

1. *Does Fairfax Cone's account of his career match your expectations of the advertising industry? Did Cone work closely with the firms he was promoting, or were there tensions between this particular advertiser and his clients? What does this say about a possible "conspiracy" between advertisers and corporate managers to control the American consumer?*

2. *Why would Bruce Barton write a book like* The Man Nobody Knows? *Why would he compare ad writers to Jesus and his disciples?*

3. *How are the print ads similar to those seen in magazines today? How are they different? What key themes and issues emerge in the print ads? Have these themes changed since the 1920s and 1930s?*

4. *Pay particular attention to the ad for Goodyear tires. This ad reflects advertisers' notion of a "democracy of goods;" namely, that we are all equal through the products (goods) that we consume. Do you agree with the message of the ad that the working-class couple on the left should be happy and content because the tires on their inexpensive car are "just the same" as those on the Rolls Royce being polished by the chauffeur? Does this ad suggest that advertisers were trying to bury class conflict (i.e., rich vs. poor) beneath a flood of consumer products? Do you see evidence today (in sneaker ads, for example) that lower-class Americans are being told that products are more important that meaningful social change?*

FURTHER READING

David M. Potter's path-breaking work, People of Plenty: Economic Abundance and the American Character *(Chicago, 1954) traces the development of the American consumer culture. Daniel Pope,* The Making of Modern Advertising *(New York, 1983), often considered one of the "standard" works of advertising history, provides a solid overview of the development of that profession, and of its effects on American society. For advertising in wartime (often simply labeled "propaganda"), see Frank W. Fox,* Madison Avenue Goes to War: The Strange Military Career of American Advertising, 1941–45 *(Provo, Utah, 1975). Stuart W. Ewen offers a harsh critique of the social impact of advertising, arguing that a conspiracy of corporate executives and ad writers distorted consumption patterns in* Captains of Consciousness: Advertising and the Social Roots of the Consumer Culture *(New York, 1976). Other useful works include Stephen Fox,* The Mirror Makers: A History of American Advertising and Its Creators *(New York, 1984), T. J. Jackson Lears,* Fables of Abundance: A Cultural History of Advertising in America *(New York, 1994), and Richard S. Tedlow,* New and Improved: The Story of Mass Marketing in America *(New York, 1990).*

The Expulsion and Relocation of Japanese Americans in World War II

Michael Les Benedict

INTRODUCTION

On 7 December 1941, following years of growing tension between Japan and the United States, Japan launched a surprise bombing of Pearl Harbor, the home port of the United States Pacific fleet. Japan's allies, Germany and Italy, quickly joined it in declaring war on the United States, bringing the Americans fully into World War II.

Claiming that Japanese and Japanese Americans on the Pacific coast were sympathetic to Japan and preparing to aid Japanese air raids and even invasion, many people there called for their expulsion from the coast. Within two months the government of the United States ordered all persons of Japanese ancestry—both aliens and "non-aliens" (that is, citizens)—to leave a large swath of territory along the Pacific coast. This included both Japanese immigrants (called Issei or "first generation") and their children (Nisei or "second generation"). The small number previously identified as pro-Japan by U.S. intelligence agencies were interned at special locations. Over 100,000 others who had nowhere to go and no means of support outside of their homes in California, western Oregon, and western Washington were expelled from the region and taken to "relocation" camps in a process military authorities called "controlled evacuation." While German Americans had been subject to harassment during World War I, and both German and Italian aliens were interned during World War II, the scope of the forced Japanese evacuation was unprecedented. Moreover, unlike German and Italian immigrants, who could acquire American citizenship after five years' residence, Japanese immigrants had been barred from acquiring American citizenship by laws that limited naturalization to white immigrants and those of African descent.

After the war, more and more Americans came to doubt the practical and legal justification for wrenching Japanese and Japanese Americans from their homes and sending them to the relocation camps. Many of the relocated Japanese were outraged; after the war some returned to Japan rather than continue to live in the United States. The vast majority who remained did little to protest their treatment after the war, but by the 1970s many Japanese Americans demanded apologies and restitution. After a long struggle, Congress passed the Civil Liberties Act of 1988, acknowledging the injustice of the "controlled evacuation" and making reparations. The readings that follow describe the evacuation and relocation program, the reaction of the people subjected to it, life in the camps, and the demand for redress.

THE JAPANESE RELOCATION: EVENTS AND ATTITUDES

Most historians have condemned the expulsion and relocation of the Japanese and Japanese Americans during World War II, attributing the decision to domestic racism, fear of the "Yellow Peril" in foreign affairs, and the hysteria surrounding the sneak attack on Pearl Harbor. But some of those who supported the evacuation policy and a few modern analysts still defend the decision. The following readings provide a more detailed account of events and their effect on the forced evacuee. The readings demonstrate the continuing disagreement over whether the policy was justified.

A Daughter of an Evacuee Describes the History of the Expulsion and Relocation

In this essay, Donna K. Nagata, whose grandparents and parents were relocated, gives an overview of the history of the evacuation. Abridged from Donna K. Nagata, Legacy of Injustice: Exploring the Cross-Generational Impact of the Japanese American Internment *(New York, 1993), 1–15.*

The Decision to Evacuate

Japanese Americans recognize February 19 as the official Day of Remembrance for the Internment. On that date in 1942, President Franklin D. Roosevelt signed Executive Order 9066, ten weeks after the Japanese attacked Pearl Harbor. The order provided the secretary of war and his designated officers with the authority to exclude all persons, both citizens and aliens, from designated areas in order to provide security against sabotage or espionage. The army took charge of implementing Executive Order 9066 by removing all Japanese Americans from the West Coast of the United States, placing them first into temporary "assembly centers" and later into concentration camps located in desolate areas of the country. No formal charges were brought against the Japanese Americans, and there was no opportunity for an individual review of their loyalty.

The stated rationale for Executive Order 9066 concerned national security; removal of Japanese Americans from the West Coast was necessary to provide safeguards against espionage or sabotage. The order was signed at a time when the military activities of Japan generated increased concern in the United States. The Japanese struck the Malay Peninsula, Hong Kong, Wake and Midway islands, and the Philippines on the same day they attacked Pearl Harbor. By the time Executive Order 9066 was signed, they had successfully taken Guam, Wake Island, most of the Philippines, and Hong Kong. Rumors that the Pearl Harbor attack had been aided by ethnic Japanese in Hawaii ran rampant in newspapers and on radio, fueled by a December 12, 1941, press report from Secretary of the Navy Frank Knox. Although Knox falsely stated that Japanese spies operated in Hawaii prior to the Pearl Harbor attack, his press statements "carried considerable weight and gave credence to the view that ethnic Japanese on the mainland were a palpable threat and danger." In an atmosphere of paranoia and general panic, Japanese American fishing boats were accused of signaling Japanese submarines with their lights, and Japanese American farmers were suspected of planting their fields in rows pointing to nearby airports.

The fears for American security were not founded on fact. Intelligence reports, including those from the Federal Bureau of Investigation (FBI) and Naval Intelligence, concluded that mass

Excerpts from "Historical Background" reprinted from *Legacy of Injustice: Exploring the Cross-Generational Impact of the Japanese American Internment* by Donna K. Nagata, published by Plenum Publishing Corporation, 1993. Copyright © 1993 by Plenum Press, a division of Plenum Publishing Corporation.

incarceration was *not* a military necessity. Indeed, many of the fears were founded in racial prejudice evident both in the public and within the military itself. The views of Lieutenant General John L. DeWitt, who recommended the exclusion of Japanese from the West Coast, illustrate the extremity of this prejudice. DeWitt was in charge of West Coast security under Secretary of War Henry L. Stimson. Encouraged by both Major General Allen W. Gullion, the provost marshal for the army, and Colonel Karl R. Bendetsen, chief of Gullion's Aliens Division, he pressured the Department of Justice to adopt stricter enemy alien controls and informed Secretary of War Stimson that there were "indications that ethnic Japanese were organized and ready for concerted action within the United States." DeWitt saw the evacuation as a military necessity because he saw no distinction between the Japanese and Japanese Americans. Ethnic heritage alone determined one's loyalty. Transcripts of a conference between DeWitt and newspaper reporters on April 14, 1943, recorded him stating bluntly to reporters that "a Jap is a Jap" and on February 14, 1942, five days before the signing of Executive Order 9066, he stated to Secretary Stimson:

> In the war in which we are now engaged racial affinities are not severed by migration. The Japanese race is an enemy race and while many second and third generation Japanese born on United States soil, possessed of the United States citizenship, have become "Americanized," the racial strains are undiluted. That Japan is allied with Germany and Italy in this struggle is no ground for assuming that any Japanese, barred from assimilation by convention as he is, though born and raised in the United States, will not turn against this nation when the final test of loyalty comes. It follows that along the Pacific Coast over 112,000 potential enemies, of Japanese extraction, are at large today.

In an incredible "catch-22," DeWitt also noted that "the very fact that no sabotage has taken place to date is a disturbing and confirming indication that such action will be taken."

Research suggests that U.S. intelligence had monitored Japanese immigrants and their activities *before* the war, and as early as August 1941, Army Intelligence inquired about the possibility of arresting and detaining those civilians who were American citizens. Prior to Pearl Harbor there were also government officials who considered the use of Japanese in America as "barter" and "reprisal" reserves in case the United States needed to trade "prisoners of war" or wanted to ensure the humane treatment of American soldiers who were held as prisoners.

Individuals did oppose DeWitt's recommendations, but such opposition was neither unified nor focused. Both the Justice Department and J. Edgar Hoover of the FBI proposed that restrained actions would be preferable to a mass evacuation. Secretary of War Stimson, Assistant Secretary of War John J. McCloy, and Attorney General Francis Biddle also disagreed with DeWitt's plans but did not protest them vigorously. However, stronger political forces pressed for mass internment along with DeWitt.

That the motivations behind the internment could not be justified simply on the basis of military necessity was evident when contrasting the sequence of events in Hawaii with those on the mainland. The military interned only 1% of the Japanese population in Hawaii, which was significantly closer to Japan, compared with more than 90% of the Japanese Americans on the mainland. Several factors contributed to the differential treatment of the Hawaiian Japanese. Japanese Americans composed a significant portion, more than one-third, of Hawaii's population, and the territory's population was more pluralistic and ethnically tolerant than the mainland. Anti-Asian sentiment, although present, did not occur at the levels evident along the West Coast. Because they were so numerous, an internment of all Japanese Americans would severely hamper day-to-day functioning on the islands. In addition, General Delos Emmons of the War Department, the commanding general of Hawaii, urged a restrained response to the presence of ethnic Japanese, recommended that the size of the areas prohibited to Japanese Americans be reduced, and objected to the exclusion of persons not actually or potentially dangerous. The difference in treatment between the Hawaiian and mainland Japanese Americans is striking. . . .

The racism underlying the internment did not emerge suddenly, for although Executive Order 9066 may serve as an official "beginning" to the internment, decades of anti-Asian prejudice prior to World War II set the context for its inception. As [historian Roger] Daniels notes, the Japanese were initially welcomed in the mid-1800s in Hawaii as a source of cheap labor on sugar plantations. The Chinese, who had been brought earlier to Hawaii as a source of inexpensive labor, came to be seen as problematic when their numbers increased. By the 1800s, Japanese labor groups were recruited in large numbers from Hawaii to come to the mainland and work in agriculture.

As the numbers of Japanese increased on the mainland, so did the levels of prejudice and hostility around them. The media portrayed the Japanese as a "yellow peril," and by 1908, the Gentleman's Agreement (an executive agreement between the United States and Japan) restricted immigration from Japan. The Gentleman's Agreement prevented the immigration of Japanese men but did allow for a significant number of Japanese women to immigrate as picture brides and begin families in this country. However, in 1924 the Immigration Act effectively stopped all Japanese immigration until 1965. These immigration restrictions had important long-term consequences in defining the demographics of the Japanese American community, isolating Japanese couples in the United States and creating a population with "unique age distributions" and distinct age peaks for each generation. For example, by 1940 the Issei (first-generation Japanese immigrant) men were generally between the ages of 50 and 64, whereas the Issei women tended to be approximately 10 years younger. Most of their U.S.-born children (the Nisei) were born between 1918 and 1922.

Pre-World War II discrimination against the Japanese was also evident in other forms of anti-Japanese legislation. Antimiscegenation laws prohibited Japanese Americans from intermarrying with whites. In addition, Japanese were considered "aliens ineligible for citizenship," and the 1913 Alien Land Law in California (where the vast majority of mainland Japanese lived) barred such aliens from purchasing land and owning property. In fact, Japanese immigrants could not become citizens until 1952.

Economic competition fueled anti-Japanese sentiment along the West Coast prior to the war. More than 50% of all Japanese men along the West Coast made their living through agriculture, forestry, and fishing. In 1940, Japanese American farms in California, Washington, and Oregon numbered over 6,000 and comprised a total of 250,000 acres. Most were small family businesses that specialized in "a labor-intensive, high-yield agricultural technique as opposed to the resource-intensive, low-yield agriculture characteristic of American farming." Altogether, these farms were valued at $72.6 million, and the productivity of the Japanese

Soldiers guarding Japanese and Japanese-Americans at Santa Anita Park, where evictees were gathered for relocation to desert camps. (Courtesy of The National Archives.)

American farmers benefitted the West Coast. Nonetheless, their success threatened many white American groups. Fears that the Japanese farmers were driving whites out of business heightened negative feelings, as did the erroneous perception that the Japanese population was exploding and creating a "yellow peril." Records show that, in reality, the Japanese farmers in California were not displacing existing farmers.

Years of the anti-Japanese sentiment prior to World War II set the emotional and economic stage for the removal of Japanese Americans. Then came the shock of Pearl Harbor, which crystallized these views into a panic. Not surprisingly, the majority of citizens favored harsh treatment of Japanese Americans. In March 1942, the National Opinion Research Center found that a vast majority of the public supported internment. Ninety-three percent of those questioned approved of the relocation of Japanese aliens, and 60% favored the evacuation of U.S. citizens as well. Two-thirds thought that once the Japanese Americans were incarcerated, they should not be allowed to move freely within the camps, but rather they ought to be kept "under strict guard like prisoners of war." Additional polls revealed that more than half of those sampled wanted to send all Japanese Americans to Japan after the war.

Those who had typically advocated for civil rights also remained silent or endorsed the internment orders. A majority of members of the Northern California Civil Liberties Union actually *favored* the evacuation orders in the spring of 1942. Japanese Americans clearly were excluded from the moral community of most other Americans at that time. Moral exclusion occurs when "individuals or groups are perceived as *outside the boundary in which moral values, rules, and considerations of fairness apply.* Those who are morally excluded are perceived as nonentities, expendable, or undeserving; consequently, harming them appears acceptable, appropriate, or just." Japanese Americans, viewed as treacherous, racially inferior, and unassimilable, were easily excluded. On the other hand, German and Italian Americans, who were racially similar to the dominant group, much more numerous, and politically powerful, did not suffer the extreme pressures toward mass incarceration; they remained within the boundaries of inclusion.

The Evacuation Process

Pearl Harbor affected Japanese Americans immediately. On the night of December 7, 1941, the FBI arrested approximately 1,500 Issei aliens who were considered to be potentially disloyal. Virtually all the leaders of Japanese American communities were removed, often with no explanation or indication of their fate. The void in leadership within the communities left Japanese Americans with few options. . . . [T]here was no political group in the larger community to support a resistance of the internment orders. As a result, the vast majority of Japanese Americans "played a passive role—waiting to see what their government would do with them."

Initially, General DeWitt attempted to implement a plan of "voluntary" resettlement. According to the plan, Japanese Americans would be restricted from military zones of the West Coast . . . [see map] but free to move outside of those zones. Data from the U.S. army indicated that approximately 5,000 individuals chose this option and "voluntarily" migrated east between March and October of 1942, in addition to an uncounted number who fled the

West Coast between December 7, 1941, and March 1942. The plan, however, was destined to fail. It was impossible for Issei and Nisei to sell their businesses and homes quickly. Many had no funds with which to move because their monies had been frozen by the government. They feared the hostility of an unknown destination. Japanese Americans could easily be recognized wherever they went, and interior states such as Idaho and Wyoming were no more welcoming than West Coast states. Recognizing the inad-

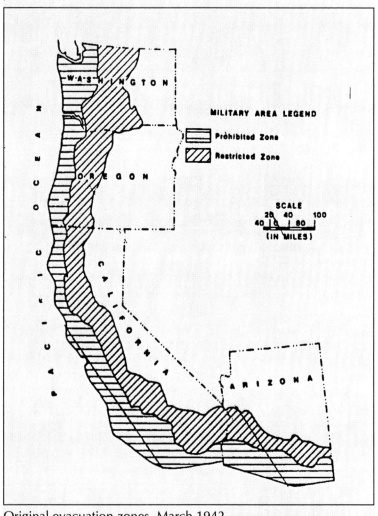

Original evacuation zones, March 1942.

equacy of the voluntary relocation program, the government took control over the evacuation process and implemented a plan for compulsory removal of Japanese Americans.

Because it was impossible to evacuate and relocate such a large group of people at the same time, the Japanese Americans first had to be transported to temporary "assembly centers." Later, when the more permanent camps were built, the internees would be moved again. The evacuation to assembly centers was carried out under military supervision of the army between March and August of 1942. Although there were Japanese Americans who were aware of the potential for some kind of evacuation, the army typically withheld details about the impending move, leaving little time or information for preparations. Many were given but a few days' notice that they would be leaving their homes. They took what they could carry. The economic losses stemming from the enforced evacuation were tremendous. Real estate, cars, appliances, farm equipment, crops ready for harvest, and personal possessions were sold for a fraction of their worth or simply left behind in haste. The fact that the military would not inform the Japanese Americans of their destination made the decision of what to bring more difficult. Families did not know whether to pack for cold or warm climates.

Throughout the evacuation families wore impersonal numbered tags. Travel by train or bus to the assembly centers was stressful and dehumanizing. Some trains had inadequate food supplies. Window shades blocked out the scenery, and passengers could not tell their whereabouts. As armed guards patrolled the trains, gossip arose that the military planned to take the Japanese Americans to an isolated area and shoot them.

After traveling hours without clear information about their destination or what fate lay in store for them, the internees arrived at the assembly centers. Sixteen of the hastily converted assembly centers were located in California, and an additional three were in Washington, Oregon, and Arizona. Many were located at race tracks and fairgrounds, where the Japanese Americans lived in horse stalls and animal quarters. Although whitewashed, they still smelled of manure. A family of eight was squeezed into a 20- by 24-foot space, four persons into an 8- by 20-foot space. Married couples often shared one large space, living in sections partitioned by a hanging sheet. Inadequate food, sanitation, and medical facilities proved equally problematic. Military police with ma-

Evicted Japanese and Japanese-Americans forced to leave the small town of Byron, California, May 2, 1942. (Courtesy of The National Archives.)

chine guns guarded the perimeter of the centers, while internal police instituted curfews, roll calls, and searches within the camps.

Although most internees lived with their families at the assembly center, others arrived without their complete family. Often, the father or husband had been taken by the FBI prior to the evacuation, but in other circumstances families were separated from loved ones who were institutionalized or incapacitated. Non-Japanese spouses of interracial couples also faced internment if they wanted to remain with their husband or wife.

Although assembly centers were labeled "temporary," the Japanese Americans remained in the centers for an average of 3 months. Then, at the end of May 1942, the process of uprooting began again. This time the long, tiresome train rides ended at the more permanent concentration camps. These 10 camps . . . were located in barren areas outside the exclusion area.

Many Japanese Americans hoped that the concentration

camps (euphemistically called "relocation centers") would provide better living conditions than the assembly centers. Unfortunately, the conditions were not significantly better. Barbed wire and armed guards persisted, as did the harsh living conditions. No camp housed less than 7,000 internees, and the largest held over 18,000. Barrack-style housing was constructed specifically for the purpose of containing the Japanese Americans. Each "block" consisted of 12 to 14 barracks, a communal mess hall, toilet and bath facilities, a laundry, and a recreation hall. A barrack measured approximately 20 by 100 feet and was divided into four to six rooms. At Topaz, a camp that was typical of the others, rooms ranged in size from 20 feet by 8 feet, to 20 feet by 24 feet. Each room contained one family. Sparse furnishings included a cot, a coal-burning stove with no coal, and a light bulb hanging from the ceiling. There was no running water. Internees braved extreme temperatures throughout the year. In the deserts, where many of the camps were located, winter temperatures could reach as low as 35 below zero and summers could be as high as 115 degrees. Dust storms arose frequently.

The War Relocation Authority (WRA), a newly formed civilian agency, was responsible for the camps. It planned to act as a facilitator of the resettlement rather than a warden for prisoners and proposed a policy that would entitle the Japanese Americans to the same treatment as other American citizens. As noted in the CWRIC [Commission on Wartime Relocation and Internment of Civilians] final report, however, the actual experience of the Japanese Americans fell far short of this initial goal. The institutional mess-hall meals were minimally adequate. Dairy items were in continual shortage, and some centers had no meat for several days each week. Facilities for the sick, elderly, and mothers with infants were particularly poor. The WRA did prepare special meals for those with health problems, but the elderly and sick who needed the special meals might have to walk a mile three times a day to get them because the meals were prepared in a building separate from the mess halls. The shortage of medical care, evident in the assembly centers, also continued. At one point, the camp in Jerome, Arkansas, had only seven doctors to provide care to 10,000 people. Epidemics of dysentery, typhoid, and tuberculosis were reported in several camps.

The Japanese Americans had meager opportunities for work while interned and performed a variety of jobs: Many worked in agriculture or food preparation, while others constructed camouflage nets or operated sawmills. According to the 1982 [CWRIC]. . . , the WRA encouraged their participation because they hoped that outsiders would view such work as a sign of Japanese American loyalty. However, a strict limit on earnings was set. Camp internees could earn no more than $19.00 a month, regardless of whether they worked as nurses or field workers. In contrast, a white WRA librarian might earn $167.00 a month in camp.

Some 30,000 Japanese American children attended public school at the time of the internment. Although inadequate numbers of textbooks, equipment, and trained teachers severely limited what could be accomplished, both the Issei and older Nisei remained committed to providing an education for the young internees. Within weeks, the Japanese American residents themselves set up kindergarten and English classes, even in the temporary assembly centers. However, once the internees were transferred to the more permanent concentration camps, the WRA made little effort to retain the educational initiatives from the assembly centers and instead instituted inadequate and paternalistic educational policies. . . . Approximately 600 Caucasian American teachers, 50 certified Japanese American teachers, and 400 Japanese American assistant teachers eventually taught in the camps.

The WRA's system of governance gave it veto power over all legislative activities. It also barred the Issei from holding elected office and created conflicts between the Issei and Nisei generations by placing greater official authority in the hands of the children and disenfranchising their parents. Such a structure directly opposed Japanese cultural values of filial piety and deference to one's elders.

Other government policies produced friction among internees. In early 1943, all Japanese Americans over age 16 in the camps were required to answer loyalty questions. These questions were to serve two purposes. First, they would be used to help camp authorities process internees requesting work furloughs and resettlement outside the camps. Second, because the government had decided to open enlistment into the armed forces to Japanese Americans in 1944, a system was needed by which "loyal" and "disloyal" Japanese could be distinguished. To accomplish this latter task, army officers and WRA staff distributed questionnaires to all draft-age males that contained two critical questions about loyalty. Question 27 asked, "Are you willing to serve in the armed forces of the United States on combat duty, wherever ordered?" Question 28 asked, "Will you swear unqualified allegiance to the United States of America and faithfully defend the United States from any or all attack by foreign or domestic forces, and forswear any form of allegiance or obedience to the Japanese emperor, or any other government, power or organization?" The answers to the required questions were then used in registering Nisei men for the draft. The Issei and women internees were required to answer loyalty questions as well, although Question 27 was rephrased to ask whether they were willing to serve in the WACS or Army Nurse Corps.

The loyalty questionnaire raised significant and painful conflicts for Issei and Nisei alike and again demonstrated the government's blatant insensitivity to the circumstances of the Japanese Americans. The Issei struggled over Question 28. To answer "yes" would require them to renounce their Japanese nationality. Yet, because they were legally prevented from becoming American citizens, this would leave them without a country of citizenship at all! On the other hand, an answer of "no" would be seen as disloyal and could lead to being transferred to another camp and separated from one's children who were citizens of the United States. The loyalty oath essentially asked the Issei to "voluntarily assume stateless status," a request that was "a clear violation of the Geneva convention."

Loyalty questions concerned the Nisei as well. Some wondered if Question 28 were a trick question, since forswearing allegiance to the emperor might also be construed as admitting that allegiance had once existed. Question 27 asked them to fight for the country that had so unjustly imprisoned them. Tensions and debates over how to respond to the loyalty questions arose between family members and friends. In the end, the majority of internees (87%) answered the question with an unqualified "yes." Qualified answers and unanswered questions were interpreted as "no's." The approximately 8,000 who answered "no" to both Question 27 and 28 were considered "disloyals" and eventually shipped to a special high-security camp at Tule Lake. There the so-called "no-no's" joined individuals who wished to expatriate or repatriate to Japan.

By January 1944, following the loyalty questionnaire, the government reinstituted the draft for Japanese Americans. According to the selective service, approximately 23,000 Nisei served during World War II. About half came from the continental United States, and among these were 2,800 Nisei inductees from the camps. Some of the young Nisei males willingly joined the armed forces. The all-Japanese American 100th Battalion and the 442nd Regimental Combat Team, composed of volunteers from Hawaii and the camps, became famous for their bravery and loyalty. Other Nisei contributed to the war effort through their service in the intelligence or by acting as interrogators of Japanese war prisoners in combat. Ironically, the Japanese heritage that made them targets for suspected disloyalty had become an asset.

Dissension and Resistance

The outstanding service record of Japanese Americans who served in the military might lead one to believe that all internees supported the recruitment effort. Other statistics, however, indicate that there were Nisei who did not accept military service as a positive alternative. Twenty-two percent of the total Nisei males eligible for the draft refused to answer "yes" to both of the loyalty questions. In addition, the army eventually recruited only 1,208 volunteers from the camps. The proportion of volunteers from the noninterned Hawaiian Japanese was significantly higher. Daniels also points out that many Japanese American soldiers who fought in Europe were farmers. White farmers of draft age would have received deferments as "essential agricultural workers," but no such occupational deferments were available to Japanese Americans. And while the 442nd Regiment and 100th Battalion were exemplary combat units, Company K, another all-Nisei unit, was plagued by low morale and insubordination. Not all Nisei welcomed the draft as a sign of reinstated rights. For them, the loyalty questionnaire and the draft represented additional insults to their citizenship and rights. At the Heart Mountain camp, some 85 men were indicted and convicted for draft resistance.

Draft resistance represented only one example of the Japanese American disillusionment. Renunciation of citizenship represented yet another. By January 1945, over 5,000 Nisei had renounced their American citizenship. Some regretted their decision several months later when an end to the war appeared near and the Justice Department announced that Nisei renunciants would be deported to Japan while their Issei parents would be relocated in the United States. Eventually, after negotiating considerable legal and bureaucratic complexities, all who wished to invalidate their renunciations were able to do so. Other Japanese Americans filed for repatriation (in the case of aliens) or expatriation (in the case of citizens) to Japan.

> In the assembly and relocation centers, applications to go to Japan had been one of the few nonviolent ways to protest degrading treatment. During three years of rising humiliation, 20,000 people chose this means to express their pain, outrage and alienation, in one of the saddest testaments to the injustice of exclusion and detection. . . . The cold statistics fail . . . to convey the scars of mind and soul that many carried with them from the camps.

As was the case with the renunciants, most repatriation and expatriation applicants eventually remained in the United States. It is nonetheless sobering that 4,724 Japanese Americans actually left the camps for Japan.

Resettlement

Beginning in 1943, Nisei who answered "yes" to the loyalty oath but did not enlist in the service began receiving clearance to leave the camps for areas outside the restricted zones of the West Coast. Resettlement was a slow process. Those who left the camps were given one-way transportation costs and $25 to begin a new life. Young Nisei between the ages of 15 and 35 relocated in cities such as Chicago, Denver, and New York and took whatever form of work they could find. Many became domestics or performed other forms of manual labor. Between 2,300 and 2,700 ended up working at Seabrook Farms in New Jersey. These individuals were influenced by farm recruiters who went to the camps to solicit resettlers by feedback from trial groups sent from the camps and letters from those already resettled in Seabrook.

Although resettlement had been a goal of the WRA from early on in the internment, there were many reasons why the Japanese Americans were reluctant to leave the camps. In addition to experiencing the physical and emotional stress of imprisonment, many were fearful to leave the camps and distrustful of resettlement offers. This was especially true of the older Issei. Government records showed that by January 1945, only one of six Issei had left the camps, and it was not until June 1946 that all camps (with the exception of Tule Lake, where hearings on detainees were held) closed. . . .

. . . Greater than two-thirds of those who left the camps eventually returned to their previous region of residence. Both those who resettled in cities away from the West Coast and those who returned to their home towns faced many adjustments. [Historian Tetsuden] Kashima, in fact, refers to the resettlement years between 1945 and 1955 as a crisis period for Japanese Americans, a time when they were forced to readjust to a normal life after the camps, find jobs and a place to live, and confront an often hostile environment. Most found their original neighborhoods greatly changed. Areas that had once been the "Japantowns" and centers of Japanese American community life had, over the war years, become occupied by other ethnic minority groups. In addition, anti-Japanese sentiments remained high, and 31 major attacks on California relocatees were reported between January and June of 1945.

We have seen that by spring of 1943, following the loyalty review of internees, there was evidence that the incarceration of the Japanese Americans was not a military necessity. Yet, many Japanese Americans remained in the camps through 1945. Why was this so? The following quote taken from the CWRIC report provides the sobering answer to this question:

> . . . the President was unwilling to act to end the exclusion until the first Cabinet meeting following the Presidential election of November, 1944. The inescapable conclusion from this . . . pattern is that the delay was motivated by political considerations. By the participants' own accounts, there is no rational explanation for maintaining the exclusion of loyal ethnic Japanese from the West Coast for eighteen months after May, 1943—except political pressure and fear.

From the beginnings of the decision to evacuate, to the closing of the camps, the Japanese Americans were the victims of racial, economic, and political injustices. By the end of the internment, with their community dispersed across the country, their lives would never be the same.

A Defense of the Relocation Policy

In the following selection, Dwight D. Murphey, a lawyer who has written on social and political philosophy, defends the relocation policy, arguing that it was justified and that conditions in the camps were good. From Dwight D. Murphey, The Dispossession of the American Indian—And Other Key Issues in American History *(Washington, D.C., 1995), 31-35, 39-41.*

On February 19, 1942, President Franklin D. Roosevelt signed Executive Order 9066. This authorized the establishment of military areas from which people of all kinds could be excluded. Lt. General John L. DeWitt was appointed the military commander to carry out the Executive Order. In March, Gen. DeWitt declared large parts of the Pacific Coast states military areas in which no one of Japanese descent would be allowed to remain. The exclusion order affected Japanese-Americans living on the West Coast by forcing them to move inland. Its only effect upon those who already lived inland was to bar them from going to the quarantined areas on the West Coast. . . .

A short-lived plan originally was to assist the Japanese-Americans in a process by which they would move inland "on their own recognizance" as individuals and families. [Karl R.] Bendetsen [who directed the evacuation for the government] says that "funds were provided for them [and] we informed them . . . where there were safe motels in which they could stay overnight." This was ended almost immediately, by late March, however . . . the need for a more organized system became apparent when most of the Japanese-Americans were not able to make arrangements to relocate quickly even with some help. A second reason was that the governors of western states (reflecting public opinion in their states) objected strongly to thousands of people of Japanese origin moving into their states without oversight. . . .

Relocated Japanese-Americans play baseball at the Lone Pine Relocation Camp, with other residents looking on. (Courtesy of The Library of Congress.)

This led to the "assembly center phase," during which the evacuees were moved to improvised centers such as race tracks and fairgrounds along the West Coast pending the construction of ten "relocation centers" in eastern California, Arizona, Utah, Idaho, Wyoming, Colorado, and as far east as Arkansas. . . .

Hastily improvised and purely temporary quarters for thousands of people who have been uprooted from their homes on short notice could not have been pleasant. There is no incongruity, however, between this and the fact, also true, that the government worked with the evacuees to take extraordinary measures to make the centers as comfortable as possible. In the short time they existed, some centers opened libraries; movies were shown regularly; there were Scout troops, arts and crafts classes, musical groups, and leagues for basketball and baseball. Three hundred and fifty people signed up for a calisthenics class at Stockton. All had playgrounds for children, and one even had a pitch-and-putt golf course. The centers were run almost entirely by the Japanese-Americans themselves.

As the ten relocation centers became ready, the evacuees were moved to them from the assembly centers. These were under the jurisdiction of the War Relocation Authority. . . . It is worth noting that no families were ever separated during the process.

As with the assembly centers, the critics find fault with much about the relocation centers. For example, the health care has been the subject of continuing dispute. Dillon Myer [director of the War Relocation Authority (WRA), which supervised the camps], however, says that "the professional care was excellent [and] was free."

There were messhalls for meals, and a large number of community enterprises, which included stores, theaters, hairdressers, community theaters, and newspapers. There was ping-pong, judo, boxing, badminton, and sumo wrestling. Again, there were basketball and baseball leagues (along with some touch football). The Santa Fe center had "gardens, two softball diamonds, two tennis courts, a miniature nine-hole golf course, a fenced forty-acre hiking area, . . . classes in calligraphy, Chinese and Japanese poetry. . . ." The Massachusetts Quakers sponsored art competitions. Libraries featured Japanese-language sections. There were chapters of the American Red Cross, YMCA, YWCA, Boy Scouts, and Girl Scouts. State Shinto, with its emperor-worship, was barred, but otherwise the evacuees worshiped as they pleased. The government paid a salary equal to an American soldier's pay ($21 per month) to those who worked in the centers.

Each of the camps (except Tule Lake . . .) had fully accredited schools through the high school level. There were nursery schools, kindergarten, the teaching of instrumental music, school choruses, achievement testing, high school newspapers and annuals, dances, active Parent-Teacher Associations, student councils and class officers. . . .

Much of the credit for the livability of the centers goes to the Japanese-Americans themselves, whose energy and intelligence immediately made the best of the situation. This was accomplished in an active relationship with the WRA.

Subject to a veto that the WRA could exercise, each relocation center was governed internally (as had been the assembly centers) by the Japanese-Americans themselves, who elected representatives from each block.

Even before the relocation centers became filled, college-age students began to leave to attend American universities. By the beginning of the fall semester in 1942, approximately 250 students had left for school, attending 143 colleges and universities. By the time the war was over, 4,300 college-age students were attending more than 300 universities around the country (though not on the West Coast). Scholarships were granted based on financial ability. Foundations and churches funded a "National Japanese American Student Relocation Council" to help with college attendance.

The centers were intended, as their name suggests, to be places in which the evacuees could stay while they were being relocated around the country. Myer says "never was there any policy of confinement for the duration." . . . That is why the camps were called "relocation centers" rather than "internment camps."

Many of the evacuees, however, remained in the centers for the duration of the war. Critics attribute this to a lack of alternatives, as though the evacuees were trapped, but Bendetsen credits the fact that life was acceptable within the centers. "Many elected to stay in the relocation centers while being gainfully employed in nearby pursuits in the general economy . . . The climate of hostility which presented intractable problems in the very early phases had long since subsided." . . .

The critics of the evacuation often argue that there was no demonstrated military necessity for it. The Report of the Commission on Wartime Relocation speaks of "the clamor" by California officials for protective action, and says that "these opinions were not informed by any knowledge of actual military risks." The extensive critical literature mocks the perception of danger, suggesting that it was a figment of hysterical imaginations.

But this is nonsense. The danger was apparent to anyone who considered the situation. Earl Warren, as attorney general of California, testified before a select committee of Congress (the "Tolan Committee") on February 21, 1942, and submitted letters from a number of local officials. Some pointed to the vulnerability of the water supply and of the large-scale irrigation systems: "It would be absolutely humanly impossible," one of them wrote, "for the small force now available in the sheriff's office to make even a pretense of guarding this tremendous farm territory and the irrigation system." Another pointed out that "a systematic campaign of incendiarism would cause terrific disaster" during the California dry season from May until October. . . .

In addition to the civilian population, there was much that was important militarily and economically along the West Coast; it was clearly exposed; and there were few means to defend it. This was enough in itself to create a critical emergency, to be met as humanely but as effectively as possible. It should not be necessary for the American government to have known specifically of plans for espionage and sabotage.

Just the same, there *was* definitive evidence of Japan's intent to exploit (and actual exploitation of) the situation. On December 4, 1941, the Office of Naval Intelligence reported a Japanese "intelligence machine geared for war, in operation, and utilizing west coast Japanese." On January 21, 1942, a bulletin from Army Intelligence "stated flat out that the Japanese government's espionage net containing Japanese aliens, first and second generation Japanese and other nationals is now thoroughly organized and working underground," according to the testimony of David D. Lowman, a retired career intelligence officer who has written extensively on declassified intelligence from World War II. . . .

Amazingly, the Commission ignored the most important source of information about espionage, which is the dispatches sent by the Japanese government to its own officials before and during the war. U. S. Navy codebreakers had broken the Japanese diplomatic code in 1938, and the decoded messages were distributed, on a basis "higher than Top Secret," to a small handful of the very highest American officials under the codename "MAGIC." Lowman testified in 1984 that "included among the diplomatic communications were hundreds of reports dealing with espionage activities in the United States and its possessions." . . .

Several officials within the Roosevelt administration opposed the evacuation of the Japanese-Americans from the West Coast, but Lowman makes a telling point: that the President, the Secretary of War, the Army Chief of Staff, the Director of Military Intelligence, the Secretary of the Navy, the Chief of Naval Operations, the Director of Naval Intelligence, and the Chiefs of Army and Navy Plans—all of whom received MAGIC—*favored* evacuation. It was those who did not have knowledge of the Japanese dispatches who found it possible, somewhat incongruously in light of the self-evident factors I have mentioned, to doubt the military necessity.

Questions

1. *What role did racism play in encouraging the government to order the forced relocation of Japanese and Japanese Americans from the Pacific coast? Do you think that military necessity alone can explain the decision? Do you think that government officials' perception of military necessity alone can explain the decision?*

2. *Does Dwight Murphey's justification of the expulsion and relocation policy help you to understand the feelings of those who supported it in 1941?*

3. *How persuasive do you find Murphey's defense of the government's policy? Did the fears and evidence of Japanese disloyalty that Murphey describes justify mass relocation? Explain.*

4. *Defenders of the evacuation of Japanese Americans from the Pacific coast describe their transfer to the relocation camps as "voluntary." Nagata, like many who have described the events, refers to the relocation as "internment," suggesting the transfer was involuntary. How voluntary does it appear to have been? If you are unsure, keep this question in mind as you read the original documents that follow.*

5. *Defenders of the evacuation and relocation policy point out that Japanese and Japanese Americans were treated much better than enemy aliens in Germany and Japan. How does this affect your evaluation of the expulsion and relocation policy?*

THE JAPANESE RELOCATION: DOCUMENTS AND FIRST-HAND ACCOUNTS

After their release from the relocation camps, few of the residents were willing to describe their experiences. For some the memory was too painful. Many adult Japanese considered their time in the camps to be a mark of shame, to be hidden. Moreover, many Japanese and Japanese Americans had been taught not to express anger openly. But over time, Japanese Americans—especially the younger generation—began to describe their experiences and express their outrage. The following documents and first-hand accounts describe their experiences and the actions of the United States government.

Executive Order 9066

After several months of debate within his administration, on 19 February 1942, President Franklin D. Roosevelt signed an executive order authorizing the military to relocate the Japanese and Japanese Americans living on the West coast. Did the president allege any actual evidence of sabotage or disloyalty? Excerpted from U.S. House of Representatives, Report of the Select Committee Investigating National Defense Migration *(hereafter cited as* Tolan Committee*),* House Report No. 2124, 77th Cong., 2d sess. (1942), 314.

WHEREAS the successful prosecution of the war requires every possible protection against espionage and against sabotage to national defense material, national defense premises, and national defense utilities. . . .

Now, THEREFORE, by virtue of the authority vested in me as President of the United States, and Commander in Chief of the Army and Navy, I hereby authorize and direct the Secretary of War, and the Military Commanders who he may from time to time designate, whenever he or any designated Commander deems such action necessary or desirable, to prescribe military areas in such places and of such extent as he or the appropriate Military Commander may determine, from which any or all persons may be excluded, and with respect to which, the right of any person to enter, remain in, or leave shall be subject to whatever restrictions the Secretary of War or the appropriate Military Commander may impose in his discretion. The Secretary of War is hereby authorized to provide for residents of any such area who are excluded therefrom, such transportation, food, shelter, and other accommodations as may be necessary, in the judgment of the Secretary of War or the said Military Commander, and until other arrangements are made, to accomplish the purpose of this order.

An Evacuation Order

The following was the first of the evacuation orders that forced over 100,000 Japanese Americans from their homes on the West coast and led to their relocation to camps in the interior. Abridged from Tolan Committee, House Report No. 2124, 332–33.

CIVILIAN EXCLUSION ORDER NO. 1
HEADQUARTERS, WESTERN DEFENSE COMMAND AND FOURTH ARMY, *Presidio of San Francisco, California, March 24, 1942.*

1. Pursuant to the provisions of Public Proclamations Nos. 1 and 2, this headquarters, dated March 2, 1942, and March 16, 1942, respectively, it is hereby ordered that all persons of Japanese ancestry, including aliens and nonaliens, be excluded from that portion of Military Area No. 1 described as "Bainbridge Island," in the State of Washington,

on or before 12 o'clock noon, P. W. T., of the 30th day of March 1942.

2. Such exclusion will be accomplished in the following manner:

   (a) Such persons may, with permission, on or prior to March 29, 1942, proceed to any approved place of their choosing beyond the limits of Military Area No. 1 and the prohibited zones established by said proclamations or hereafter similarly established, subject only to such regulations as to travel and change of residence as are now or may hereafter be prescribed by this headquarters and by the United States Attorney General. Persons affected hereby will not be permitted to take up residence or remain within the region designated as Military Area No. 1 or the prohibited zones heretofore or hereafter established. Persons affected hereby are required on leaving or entering Bainbridge Island to register and obtain a permit at the Civil Control Office to be established on said Island at or near the ferryboat landing.

   (b) On March 30, 1942, all such persons who have not removed themselves from Bainbridge Island in accordance with Paragraph 1 hereof shall, in accordance with instructions of the Commanding General, Northwestern Sector, report to the Civil Control Office referred to above on Bainbridge Island for evacuation in such manner and to such place or places as shall then be prescribed.

   (c) A responsible member of each family affected by this order and each individual living alone so affected will report to the Civil Control Office described above between 8 a. m. and 5 p. m. Wednesday, March 25, 1942.

3. Any person affected by this order who fails to comply with any of its provisions or who is found on Bainbridge Island after 12 o'clock noon, P. W. T., of March 30, 1942, will be subject to the criminal penalties provided by Public Law No. 503, 77th Congress, approved March 21, 1942, entitled "An Act to Provide a Penalty for Violation of Restrictions or Orders with Respect to Persons Entering, Remaining in, Leaving, or Committing Any Act in Military Areas or

Zone", and alien Japanese will be subject to immediate apprehension and internment.

J. L. DE WITT,
Lieutenant General,
U.S. Army, Commanding

The Uchida Family is Evacuated

Like many other community leaders, Yoshiko Uchida's father, Dwight Takashi Uchida, the manager of a leading department store serving the Japanese community in Berkeley, California, was arrested and interned immediately after the bombing of Pearl Harbor. His family, including his daughter Yoshiko, a student at the University of California, remained in Berkeley until ordered to evacuate on 21 April 1942. From Yoshiko Uchida, Desert Exile: The Uprooting of a Japanese American Family *(Seattle, 1982), 58–60, 62.*

Each day we watched the papers for the evacuation orders covering the Berkeley area. On April 21, the headlines read: "Japs Given Evacuation Orders Here." I felt numb as I read the front page story. "Moving swiftly, without any advance notice, the Western Defense Command today ordered Berkeley's estimated 1,319 Japanese, aliens and citizens alike, evacuated to the Tanforan Assembly Center by noon, May 1." (This gave us exactly ten days' notice.) "Evacuees will report at the Civil Control Station being set up in Pilgrim Hall of the First Congregational Church . . . between the hours of 8:00 A.M. and 5:00 P.M. next Saturday and Sunday."

This was Exclusion Order Number Nineteen, which was to uproot us from our homes and send us into the Tanforan Assembly Center in San Bruno, a hastily converted racetrack.

All Japanese were required to register before the departure date, and my sister, as head of the family, went to register for us.

Excerpts from "Evacuation" reprinted from *Desert Exile: The Uprooting of a Japanese American Family* by Yoshiko Uchida, published by the University of Washington Press, 1982. Copyright © 1982 by Yoshiko Uchida.

She came home with baggage and name tags that were to bear our family number and be attached to all our belongings. From that day on we became Family Number 13453.

Although we had been preparing for the evacuation orders, still when they were actually issued, it was a sickening shock.

"Ten days! We have only ten days to get ready!" my sister said frantically. Each day she rushed about, not only taking care of our business affairs, but, as our only driver, searching for old crates and cartons for packing, and taking my mother on various errands as well.

Mama still couldn't seem to believe that we would have to leave. "How can we clear out in ten days a house we've lived in for fifteen years?" she asked sadly.

But my sister and I had no answers for her.

Mama had always been a saver, and she had a tremendous accumulation of possessions. Her frugal upbringing had caused her to save string, wrapping paper, bags, jars, boxes, even bits of silk thread left over from sewing, which were tied end to end and rolled up into a silk ball. Tucked away in the corners of her desk and bureau drawers were such things as small stuffed animals, wooden toys, *kokeshi* dolls, marbles, and even a half-finished pair of socks she was knitting for a teddy bear's paw. Many of these were "found objects" that the child in her couldn't bear to discard, but they often proved useful in providing diversion for some fidgety visiting child. These were the simple things to dispose of.

More difficult were the boxes that contained old letters from her family and friends, our old report cards from the first grade on, dozens of albums of family photographs, notebooks and sketch pads full of our childish drawings, valentines and Christmas cards we had made for our parents, innumerable guest books filled with the signatures and friendly words of those who had once been entertained. These were the things my mother couldn't bear to throw away. Because we didn't own our house, we could leave nothing behind. We had to clear the house completely, and everything in it had either to be packed for storage or thrown out.

We surveyed with desperation the vast array of dishes, lacquerware, silverware, pots and pans, books, paintings, porcelain and pottery, furniture, linens, rugs, records, curtains, garden tools, cleaning equipment, and clothing that filled our house. We put up a sign in our window reading, "Living room sofa and chair for sale." We sold things we should have kept and packed away foolish trifles we should have discarded. We sold our refrigerator, our dining room set, two sofas, an easy chair, and a brand new vacuum cleaner with attachments. Without a sensible scheme in our heads, and lacking the practical judgment of my father, the three of us packed frantically and sold recklessly. Although the young people of our church did what they could to help us, we felt desperate as the deadline approached. Our only thought was to get the house emptied in time, for we knew the Army would not wait.

Organizations such as the First Congregational Church of Berkeley were extremely helpful in anticipating the needs of the panic-stricken Japanese and provided immediate, practical assistance. Families of the church offered storage space to those who needed it, and we took several pieces of furniture to be stored in the basement of one such home. Another non-Japanese friend offered to take our books and stored more than eight large cartons for us. In typical Japanese fashion, my mother took gifts to express her gratitude to each person who helped us. . . .

By now I had to leave the university, as did all the other Nisei students. We had stayed as long as we could to get credit for the spring semester, which was crucial for those of us who were seniors. My professors gave me a final grade on the basis of my midterm grades and the university granted all Nisei indefinite leaves of absence.

During the last few weeks on campus, my friends and I became sentimental and took pictures of each other at favorite campus sites. The war had jolted us into a crisis whose impact was too enormous for us to fully comprehend, and we needed these small remembrances of happier times to take with us as we went our separate ways to various government camps throughout California.

A Description of a Camp

Minoru Yasui, a California-born lawyer and U.S. Army reserve officer, refused to report for relocation. He was taken from his home in Oregon, interned with 3,000 other Japanese Americans in Portland for five months, and then transported to the Minidoka camp in Idaho. Abridged

The belongings of relocated Japanese and Japanese-Americans, piled behind the barbed-wire fence at the Salinas Relocation Center. (Courtesy of The Library of Congress.)

from John Tateishi, And Justice for All: An Oral History of the Japanese American Detention Camps *(New York, 1984), 76–77.*

We arrived late afternoon, at some isolated siding in the desert area, north of Twin Falls, although we did not know where we were. No houses were in sight, no trees or anything green— only scrubby sagebrush and an occasional low catcus, and mostly dry, baked earth. There was a slight rise to the north, and one could not see to the horizon.

Baggage was unloaded and piled up next to the road, and Army trucks were rolling in, kicking up huge clouds of dust. People came off the train, were lined up and loaded into the trucks, and went off into the distance. The seats were hard planks, and after riding all day on the train, most were sore and tired.

We had left the dark, dank confines of a livestock barn hoping to breathe the fresh, open air. But because the virgin desert had been bulldozed and disturbed by men and machinery, instead of fresh air, we got to breathe dust. I remember groups of women getting off the train, looking bewildered. After the lush greenness of the Willamette Valley, to see the sterile, dusty desert which was to be our home "for the duration," many sat on the baggage in the middle of nowhere and wept. . . .

We saw again the barbed-wire fences, the watchtowers, guard houses, the MP detachments, the administration housing, warehouse areas, and block after block of black, tar-paper barracks, about 120 feet long and about 20 feet wide. I remember that at least the mess halls and kitchens were completed, and that evening we had hot meals, perhaps spam and canned vegetables. The barracks were supplied with army cots with metal springs, and we got padding-filled ticks and a couple of army blankets. There was a potbellied stove, and each block had a coal depot. One bare bulb hung from the center of the room. There were real composition-board ceilings but the walls were unfinished with open two-by-four studs. The floor was wood, and single layered, so one could see the earth below, through the cracks. The smaller units for childless couples were on the end of the building, with two windows on each side, or a total of four windows. There was only one entrance to each unit. No chairs or tables were furnished; however, later the evacuees scrounged scrap lumber and built chairs, tables, bunk beds, dressers, and other things. But only those who were handy with tools could do this. The internee wives with small children were not always able to furnish their rooms comfortably. There was, however, a great deal of sharing and exchange going on.

The Loyalty Questionnaire

In February 1943 the government began to register the people it had relocated to camps. To facilitate the release of those considered loyal and to encourage loyal Japanese Americans to enlist in the armed forces, the government prepared a questionnaire to accompany registration. Question 27 asked Nisei men if they were willing to serve in the armed forces in combat wherever ordered. Question 28 amounted to a loyalty oath— asking respondents to reaffirm allegiance to the United States and renounce allegiance to Japan. In the camps, Japanese Americans divided bitterly about how to respond. In the end about 5,000 refused to take the oath of allegiance and refused to express a willingness to fight for the United States against "any or all" of its enemies, including Japan. Extremists among the refusers worked to foment resistance to American authorities among camp residents, resorting at times to violence and intimidation. The following describes how Frank Chuman, a California-born law student in the Manzanar camp in the California desert, anguished over what to do. Taken from John Tateishi, And Justice for All: An Oral History of the Japanese American Detention Camps, *230–32.*

I didn't get the full brunt of the anti-Japanese hostility which was a hell of a good thing, because when I went to Manzanar there was a delayed reaction for me. What the hell am I doing in camp? I thought. While I was very busy working in the hospital, I said to myself, Why should the United States Government doubt our loyalty to the United States? We haven't done anything to justify this kind of treatment. Certainly not myself and certainly none of the others that I know of. And yet here I am in a camp of ten thousand people—men, women, and children. So I began to think to myself, because I had studied law—constitutional law and constitutional rights and due process and equal protection and all the rest of it—Jesus Christ, we've been deprived of our constitutional rights. There's been no accusations against me, and yet I'm suspect and I'm arbitrarily told to go into a camp. It's completely in violation of my rights. . . . And I really got angry and very, very upset at the United States Government for doing this kind of thing to not only me, but all Japanese Americans. I really got upset.

The Army recruiting team came into Manzanar around the early part of 1943. We had a big meeting in this mess hall of all persons eligible for military duty with two white soldiers and a person of Japanese ancestry, and this guy was trying to persuade us all to volunteer for the Army, and I'm not too sure whether I got up and spoke back to him or whether I said it in my own mind, but I said, "Why should we fight for the United States Government as soldiers, when the United States Government distrusts us? Why do they now want us to serve when they consider us to be disloyal? Why do they want us to serve when they have taken us out of our homes and schools and businesses, and now they want us to become loyal to the United States? It doesn't make sense, and so far as I'm concerned I'm not going to do anything to go into the

United States Army until the United States Government does something to remedy this unjust situation." I cannot remember whether I stood up and said it or whether I felt it.

In any event, that's the way it was. In the latter part of 1943, this questionnaire came out sponsored by the WRA, and in that questionnaire it had something like "request for relocation" as well as the questionnaire. It was in two parts. And there were these questions 27 and 28, "Are you willing to foreswear any allegiance to any foreign potentate and say that you are loyal to the United States?" and, "Are you willing to bear arms for the United States?" The first answer that I gave to both questions was no. I was so goddamned mad at that questionnaire. It was insulting, impugning without any evidence, just from the top down that there was something that made us Japanese Americans suspect in loyalty, allegiance, that we wouldn't fight for the government and saying now you're going to fight. They don't have to push it down my throat—are you willing to bear arms to defend the United States? That's so goddamned obvious that I would do that that it just really made me angry. . . .

I did not remain a no-no, because all of a sudden I thought to myself, after I had said that, I regretted it, because it wasn't my true feelings. There was no way that I could hate the United States Government, but I was goddamned angry at them for doing things like that about us.

The Supreme Court Upholds Japanese Relocation: *Korematsu* v. *U.S.* (1944)

Several Japanese Americans resisted the government exclusion orders in order to challenge their constitutionality in the courts. In 1943 the Supreme Court sustained a curfew applying to all people of Japanese ancestry along the Pacific Coast. A year later, to the dismay of civil libertarians, it upheld Executive Order 9066 and the relocation program instituted under its authority. Abridged from Korematsu v. U.S., 323 US 214, (1944), 216, 218–20, 233–34, 240, 242.

Opinion of the Court

It should be noted, to begin with, that all legal restrictions which curtail the civil rights of a single racial group are immediately suspect. That is not to say that all such restrictions are unconstitutional. It is to say that courts must subject them to the most rigid scrutiny. Pressing public necessity may sometimes justify the existence of such restrictions; racial antagonism never can. . . .

. . . [E]xclusion of those of Japanese origin was deemed necessary because of the presence of an unascertained number of disloyal members of the group, most of whom we have no doubt were loyal to this country. It was because we could not reject the finding of the military authorities that it was impossible to bring about an immediate segregation of the disloyal from the loyal that we sustained the validity of the curfew order as applying to the whole group. In the instant case, temporary exclusion of the entire group was rested by the military on the same ground. The judgment that exclusion of the whole group was for the same reason a military imperative answers the contention that the exclusion was in the nature of group punishment based on antagonism to those of Japanese origin. . . .

We uphold the exclusion order as of the time it was made and when the petitioner violated it. . . . In doing so, we are not unmindful of the hardships imposed by it upon a large group of American citizens. . . . Citizenship has its responsibilities as well as its privileges, and in time of war the burden is always heavier. Compulsory exclusion of large groups of citizens from their homes, except under circumstances of direst emergency and peril, is inconsistent with our basic governmental institutions. But when under conditions of modern warfare our shores are threatened by hostile forces, the power to protect must be commensurate with the threatened danger. . . .

MR. JUSTICE MURPHY, dissenting.
This exclusion of "all persons of Japanese ancestry, both alien and non-alien," from the Pacific Coast area on a plea of military necessity in the absence of martial law ought not to be approved. Such exclusion goes over "the very brink of constitutional power" and falls into the ugly abyss of racism. . . .

. . . [I]t is essential that there be definite limits to military discretion, especially where martial law has not been declared.

Individuals must not be left impoverished of their constitutional rights on a plea of military necessity that has neither substance nor support. . . .

. . . No one denies, of course, that there were some disloyal persons of Japanese descent on the Pacific Coast who did all in their power to aid their ancestral land. Similar disloyal activities have been engaged in by many persons of German, Italian and even more pioneer stock in our country. But to infer that examples of individual disloyalty prove group disloyalty and justify discriminatory action against the entire group is to deny that under our system of law individual guilt is the sole basis for deprivation of rights. . . . To give constitutional sanction to that inference in this case, however well intentioned may have been the military command on the Pacific Coast is to adopt one of the cruelest of the rationales used by our enemies to destroy the dignity of the individual and to encourage and open the door to discriminatory actions against other minority groups in the passions of tomorrow. . . .

. . . All residents of this nation are kin in some way by blood or culture to a foreign land. Yet they are primarily and necessarily a part of the new and distinct civilization of the United States. They must accordingly be treated at all times as the heirs of the American experiment and as entitled to all the rights and freedoms guaranteed by the Constitution.

The Government Reinvestigates

In response to agitation by Japanese Americans in the 1970s and renewed public interest in the events surrounding Japanese exclusion and relocation, Congress established a commission to investigate the subject. After taking testimony from those who organized and administered the program, those subjected to it, and historians of it, the Commission concluded that the exclusion and relocation had been unjustified and unjustifiable. It recommended a formal apology and restitution. Excerpted from Personal Justice Denied: Report of the Commission on Wartime Relocation and Internment of Civilians *(Washington, D.C., 1982), 2–3, 18.*

This policy of exclusion, removal and detention was executed against 120,000 people without individual review, and exclusion was continued virtually without regard for their demonstrated loyalty to the United States. Congress was fully aware of and supported the policy of removal and detention; it sanctioned the exclusion by enacting a statue which made criminal the violation of orders issued pursuant to Executive Order 9066. The United States Supreme Court held the exclusion constitutionally permissible in the context of war, but struck down the incarceration of admittedly loyal American citizens on the ground that it was not based on statutory authority.

All this was done despite the fact that not a single documented act of espionage, sabotage or fifth column activity was committed by an American citizen of Japanese ancestry or by a resident Japanese alien on the West Coast.

No mass exclusion or detention, in any part of the country, was ordered against American citizens of German or Italian descent. Official actions against enemy aliens of other nationalities were much more individualized and selective than those imposed on the ethnic Japanese.

The exclusion, removal and detention inflicted tremendous human cost. There was the obvious cost of homes and businesses sold or abandoned under circumstances of great distress, as well as injury to careers and professional advancement. But, most important, there was the loss of liberty and the personal stigma of suspected disloyalty for thousands of people who knew themselves to be devoted to their country's cause and to its ideals but whose repeated protestations of loyalty were discounted—only to be demonstrated beyond any doubt by the record of Nisei solders, who returned from the battlefields of Europe as the most decorated and distinguished combat unit of World War II, and by the thousands of other Nisei who served against the enemy in the Pacific, mostly in military intelligence. The wounds of the exclusion and detention have healed in some respects, but the scars of that experience remain, painfully real in the minds of those who lived through the suffering and deprivation of the camps.

The personal injustice of excluding, removing and detaining loyal American citizens is manifest. Such events are extraordinary and unique in American history. For every citizen and for American public life, they pose haunting questions about our country and its past. . . .

The promulgation of Executive Order 9066 was not justified by military necessity, and the decisions which followed from it— detention, ending detention and ending exclusion—were not driven by analysis of military conditions. The broad historical causes which shaped these decisions were race prejudice, war hysteria and a failure of political leadership. Widespread ignorance of Japanese Americans contributed to a policy conceived in haste and executed in an atmosphere of fear and anger at Japan. A grave injustice was done to American citizens and resident aliens of Japanese ancestry who, without individual review or any probative evidence against them, were excluded, removed and detained by the United States during World War II.

The Civil Liberties Act of 1988

In response to the report of the Commission on Wartime Relocation and Internment of Civilians, on 10 August 1988, Congress passed the Civil Liberties Act of 1988. The act requested the president to issue pardons to those convicted of violating the curfew, exclusion, and relocation orders; authorized restitution in the amount of $20,000 to every person expelled, interned, or relocated; and set up a fund to finance educational programs to inform the public about the expulsion and relocation "so as to prevent the recurrence of any similar event." Taken from U.S. Statutes at Large, *vol. 102, 1988 (1990), 903–4.*

SEC. 2. STATEMENT OF THE CONGRESS.

(a) WITH REGARD TO INDIVIDUALS OF JAPANESE ANCESTRY.—The Congress recognizes that, as described by the Commission on Wartime Relocation and Internment of Civilians, a grave injustice was done to both citizens and permanent resident aliens of Japanese ancestry by the evacuation, relocation, and internment of civilians during World War II. As the Commission documents, these actions were carried out without adequate security reasons and without any acts of espionage or sabotage documented by the Commission, and were motivated largely by racial prejudice, wartime hysteria, and a failure of political leadership. The excluded individuals of Japanese ancestry suffered enormous damages, both material and intangible, and there were incalculable losses in education and job training, all of which resulted in significant human suffering for which appropriate compensation has not been made. For these fundamental violations of the basic civil liberties and constitutional rights of these individuals of Japanese ancestry, the Congress apologizes on behalf of the Nation.

Questions

---

1. *Many non-Japanese tried to help their Japanese and Japanese American neighbors as they were forced to leave the Pacific Coast. Should they have done more? What more could they have done?*

2. *Should the Nisei have resisted the relocation program more forcefully? What might have inhibited such resistance?*

3. *Why did some of the Japanese and Japanese Americans in the relocation camps refuse to reaffirm their allegiance to the United States and refuse to agree to fight in the armed forces when presented with Questions 27 and 28 of the registration questionnaire in 1943? How would you have answered the questions?*

4. *On what basis did the Supreme Court sustain the constitutionality of Japanese expulsion and relocation in* Korematsu v. U.S.? *On what basis did Justice Murphy disagree? Do you think an occurrence similar to Japanese relocation could take place in a future time of war? Do you think the Supreme Court might intervene?*

5. *Do you think it was appropriate for Congress to apologize formally for the actions taken during World War II? Do you think the formal apology and the Civil Liberties Act might deter similar actions by government in the future? Explain.*

FURTHER READING

Page Smith, Democracy on Trial: The Japanese American Evacuation and Relocation in World War Two *(New York, 1995) is a balanced chronicle of the events leading up to the relocation of the Japanese and their experiences afterwards. Smith argues that perceived military necessity, rather than racism, motivated the government's decision. Roger Daniels takes the opposite view in* Concentration Camps USA: Japanese Americans and World War II *(New York, 1971). In* Justice at War *(New York, 1983), Peter H. Irons also argues that political considerations and the racism of the Pacific coast military leaders overcame the resistance to relocation on the part of some officials of the Roosevelt administration. John Tateishi compiled the remembrances of camp inmates in* And Justice for All: An Oral History of the Japanese American Detention Camps *(New York, 1984).* Righting a Wrong: Japanese Americans and the Passage of the Civil Liberties Act of 1988 *(Stanford, California, 1993), by Leslie T. Hatamiya, tells how crusaders secured compensation and the official apology of the United States government for its treatment of Japanese American citizens during World War II. Lillian Baker trenchantly defends the expulsion and relocation policy in* American and Japanese Relocation in World War II: Fact, Fiction & Fallacy *(Medford, Oregon, 1990).*

The Origins of the Cold War

Peter L. Hahn,
Michael J. Hogan, and Bruce Karhoff

INTRODUCTION

During World War II the United States and the Soviet Union overcame their traditional discord and cooperated to defeat Germany and Japan. The end of the war in 1945, however, eliminated the original reason for American-Soviet cooperation and opened an era of profound tension between the two victorious allies. The United States and the Soviet Union vied for political and economic influence in a postwar world beset by massive physical destruction, political instability, and vacuums of power in the regions formerly dominated by Germany and Japan. A series of conflicts and crises ensued over issues such as the form of government in Poland, the political and economic orientation of Germany, the level of U.S. and Soviet military involvement in Europe, the control of atomic weapons, and the outcome of civil wars in Greece, China, and Korea. By 1950, the great powers had divided Europe into eastern and western spheres of influence in political, economic, and military matters. Tensions escalated sharply after June 1950, when U.S. forces intervened to repulse a major offensive by Communist North Korea against non-Communist South Korea. Such conflicts caused the Cold War, an American-Soviet confrontation that lasted for nearly fifty years.

THE CONTEMPORARY DEBATE
OVER THE COLD WAR

The documents printed in this section shed light on several dimensions of the early Cold War. They illustrate some of the ideas that gave birth to the United States's policy of containment of the Soviet Union and the evolution of that policy from 1946 to 1950. They also reveal some of the opposition to this policy on the American side and provide a glimpse of the Soviet view of global affairs in general and of the Truman Doctrine of 1947 in particular. Collectively, the records printed below demonstrate the multilayered and constantly changing dynamics of the early Cold War conflict.

Stalin Suggests that Conflict Is Inevitable

On February 9, 1946, Soviet leader Josef Stalin delivered a public address in which he blamed World War II on international capitalism and celebrated Soviet contributions to the defeat of Germany. Published during a time of mounting East-West tensions over territorial issues in Eastern Europe and the Middle East, the speech provoked substantial concern in the United States that Stalin was mobilizing his people for conflict—possibly even war—with the West. Excerpted from Text of a Speech Delivered By J. V. Stalin at an Election Rally in Stalin Electoral Area, Moscow, February 9, 1946 *(Washington, 1946), 3, 5–8, 13–15.*

Comrades!

. . . It would be wrong to think that the Second World War was a casual occurrence or the result of mistakes of any particular statesmen, though mistakes undoubtedly were made. Actually, the war was the inevitable result of the development of world economic and political forces on the basis of modern monopoly capitalism. Marxists have declared more than once that the capitalist system of world economy harbors elements of general crises and armed conflicts and that, hence, the development of world capitalism in our time proceeds not in the form of smooth and even progress but through crises and military catastrophes.

The fact is, that the unevenness of development of the capitalist countries usually leads in time to violent disturbance of equilibrium in the world system of capitalism, that group of capitalist countries which considers itself worse provided than others with raw materials and markets usually making attempts to alter the situation and repartition the "spheres of influence" in its favor by armed force. The result is a splitting of the capitalist world into two hostile camps and war between them.

. . . And so, what are the results of the war?

There is one chief result in which all other results have their source. This result is that in the upshot of the war our enemies were defeated and we, together with our Allies, emerged the victors. We concluded the war with complete victory over the enemies. That is the chief result of war. . . . In order to grasp the great historic importance of our victory we must examine the thing more concretely.

And so, how is our victory over our enemies to be understood? . . .

Our victory means, first of all, that our Soviet social order has triumphed, that the Soviet social order has successfully passed the ordeal in the fire of war and has proved its unquestionable vitality.

. . . Second, our victory means that our Soviet state system has triumphed, that our multinational Soviet State has stood all the trials of war and has proved its vitality.

. . . Third, our victory means that the Soviet armed forces have triumphed, that our Red Army has triumphed, that the Red Army bore up heroically under all the trials of war, utterly routed the armies of our enemies and came out of the war as a victor.

. . . The war showed that the Red Army is not a "colossus with feet of clay," but a first-class contemporary army with fully mod-

Reprinted from *Information Bulletin:* Embassy of the Union of Soviet Socialist Republics, Washington, D.C., March 1946.

ern armaments, highly experienced commanding personnel and high moral and fighting qualities. It must not be forgotten that the Red Army is the army that utterly routed the German army which but yesterday was striking terror into the armies of the European states.

. . . Now a few words about the Communist Party's plans of work for the immediate future. As is known these plans are set forth in the new Five-Year Plan which is shortly to be endorsed. The principal aims of the new Five-Year Plan are to rehabilitate the ravaged areas of the country, to restore the prewar level in industry and agriculture, and then to surpass this level in more or less substantial measure. To say nothing of the fact that the rationing system will shortly be abolished *(stormy, prolonged applause)*, special attention will be devoted to extending the production of consumer goods, to raising the living standard of the working people by steadily lowering the prices of all goods *(stormy, prolonged applause)*, and to the widespread construction of all manner of scientific research institutions *(applause)* that can give science the opportunity to develop its potentialities. *(Stormy applause.)*

. . . As regards the plans for a longer period ahead, the Party means to organize a new mighty upsurge in the national economy, which would allow us to increase our industrial production, for example, three times over as compared with the prewar period. . . .

In conclusion, allow me to thank you for the confidence you have shown me *(prolonged, unabating applause. Shout from the audience: "Hurrah for the great captain of all victories, Comrade Stalin!")* in nominating me to the Supreme Soviet. You need not doubt that I shall do my best to justify your trust.

Kennan Warns of Russian Expansion

Alarmed by Stalin's speech, the State Department instructed its leading Soviet expert, George F. Kennan, chargé d'affaires at the U.S. embassy in Moscow, to assess the speech's significance and to predict future Soviet behavior. Kennan replied by sending the so-called long telegram, a secret cable that summarized the principles of Soviet foreign policy, anticipated substantial Soviet efforts to expand political and economic influence around the world by overt and covert methods, and suggested peaceful but firm U.S. resistance to such expansionism. Kennan's arguments, which he also published under a pseudonym in Foreign Affairs *in July 1947, formed the basis of President Truman's policy of containment of the Soviet Union. Excerpted from U.S. Department of State,* Foreign Relations of the United States, 1946 *(Washington, 1969), 6:697–99, 701–9.*

Basic Features of Post War Soviet Outlook, as Put Forward by Official Propaganda Machine, Are as Follows:

(a) USSR still lives in antagonistic "capitalist encirclement" with which in the long run there can be no permanent peaceful coexistence. As stated by Stalin in 1927 to a delegation of American workers:

> "In course of further development of international revolution there will emerge two centers of world significance: a socialist center, drawing to itself the countries which tend toward socialism, and a capitalist center, drawing to itself the countries that incline toward capitalism. Battle between these two centers for command of world economy will decide fate of capitalism and of communism in entire world."

(b) Capitalist world is beset with internal conflicts, inherent in nature of capitalist society. These conflicts are insoluble by means of peaceful compromise. Greatest of them is that between England and US.

(c) Internal conflicts of capitalism inevitably generate wars. Wars thus generated may be of two kinds: intra-capitalist wars between two capitalist states, and wars of intervention against socialist world. Smart capitalists, vainly seeking escape from inner conflicts of capitalism, incline toward latter.

(d) Intervention against USSR, while it would be disastrous to those who undertook it, would cause renewed delay in progress of Soviet socialism and must therefore be forestalled at all costs.

(e) Conflicts between capitalist states, though likewise fraught with danger for USSR, nevertheless hold out great possibilities for advancement of socialist cause, particularly if USSR remains militarily powerful, ideologically monolithic and faithful to its present brilliant leadership.

. . . So much for premises. To what deductions do they lead from standpoint of Soviet policy? To following:

(a) Everything must be done to advance relative strength of USSR as factor in international society. Conversely, no opportunity must be missed to reduce strength and influence, collectively as well as individually, of capitalist powers.

(b) Soviet efforts, and those of Russia's friends abroad, must be directed toward deepening and exploiting of differences and conflicts between capitalist powers. If these eventually deepen into an "imperialist" war, this war must be turned into revolutionary upheavals within the various capitalist countries.

(c) "Democratic-progressive" elements abroad are to be utilized to maximum to bring pressure to bear on capitalist governments along lines agreeable to Soviet interests.

(d) Relentless battle must be waged against socialist and social-democratic leaders abroad. . . .

Background of Outlook

Before examining ramifications of this party line in practice there are certain aspects of it to which I wish to draw attention.

First, it does not represent natural outlook of Russian people. . . . But party line is binding for outlook and conduct of people who make up apparatus of power—party, secret police and Government—and it is exclusively with these that we have to deal.

Second, please note that premises on which this party line is based are for most part simply not true. Experience has shown that peaceful and mutually profitable coexistence of capitalist and socialist states is entirely possible. . . .

Nevertheless, all these theses, however baseless and disproven, are being boldly put forward again today. What does this indicate? It indicates that Soviet party line is not based on any objective analysis of situation beyond Russia's borders: that it has, indeed, little to do with conditions outside of Russia; that it arises mainly from basic inner-Russian necessities which existed before recent war and exist today.

At bottom of Kremlin's neurotic view of world affairs is traditional and instinctive Russian sense of insecurity. Originally, this was insecurity of a peaceful agricultural people trying to live on vast exposed plain in neighborhood of fierce nomadic peoples. To this was added, as Russia came into contact with economically advanced West, fear of more competent, more powerful, more highly organized societies in that area. . . . For this reason they have always feared foreign penetration, feared direct contact between Western world and their own, feared what would happen if Russians learned truth about world without or if foreigners learned truth about world within. And they have learned to seek security only in patient but deadly struggle for total destruction of rival power, never in compacts and compromises with it. . . .

Projection of Soviet Outlook in Practical Policy on Official Level

. . . (a) Internal policy devoted to increasing in every way strength and prestige of Soviet state: intensive military-industrialization; maximum development of armed forces; great displays to impress outsiders; continued secretiveness about internal matters, designed to conceal weaknesses and to keep opponents in dark.

(b) Wherever it is considered timely and promising, efforts will be made to advance official limits of Soviet power. . . .

(c) Russians will participate officially in international organizations where they see opportunity of extending Soviet power or of inhibiting or diluting power of others. . . .

(d) Toward colonial areas and backward or dependent peoples, Soviet policy, even on official plane, will be directed toward weakening of power and influence and contacts of advanced Western nations, on theory that in so far as this policy is successful, there will be created a vacuum which will favor Communist-Soviet penetration. . . .

Basic Soviet Policies on Unofficial, or Subterranean Plane . . .

Agencies utilized for promulgation of policies on this plane are following:
1. Inner central core of Communist Parties in other countries . . . tightly coordinated and directed by Moscow. . . .
2. Rank and file of Communist Parties. . . . no longer even taken into confidence about realities of movement. . . .
3. A wide variety of national associations or bodies which can be dominated or influenced. . . . These include: labor

      unions, youth leagues, women's organizations, racial soci-
      eties, religious societies, social organizations, cultural
      groups, liberal magazines, publishing houses, etc.

4.   International organizations which can be similarly pen-
      etrated through influence over various national compo-
      nents. Labor, youth and women's organizations are promi-
      nent among them. . . .

It may be expected that component parts of this far-flung apparatus will be utilized . . . as follows:

(a) To undermine general political and strategic potential of major western powers. Efforts will be made in such countries to disrupt national self confidence, to hamstring measures of national defense, to increase social and industrial unrest, to stimulate all forms of disunity. . . . Here poor will be set against rich, black against white, young against old, newcomers against established residents, etc.

(b) On unofficial plane particularly violent efforts will be made to weaken power and influence of Western Powers of [on] colonial backward, or dependent peoples. On this level, no holds will be barred. . . .

(c) Where individual governments stand in path of Soviet purposes pressure will be brought for their removal from office. . . .

(d) In foreign countries Communists will, as a rule, work toward destruction of all forms of personal independence, economic, political or moral. . . .

(e) Everything possible will be done to set major Western Powers against each other. . . .

(f) In general, all Soviet efforts on unofficial international plane will be negative and destructive in character, designed to tear down sources of strength beyond reach of Soviet control. . . . The Soviet regime is a police regime par excellence, reared in the dim half world of Tsarist police intrigue, accustomed to think primarily in terms of police power. This should never be lost sight of in gauging Soviet motives. . . .

Practical Deductions from Standpoint of U S Policy

In summary, we have here a political force committed fanatically to the belief that with US there can be no permanent *modus vivendi*, that it is desirable and necessary that the internal harmony of our society be disrupted, our traditional way of life be destroyed, the international authority of our state be broken, if Soviet power is to be secure. . . . This is admittedly not a pleasant picture. Problem of how to cope with this force in [*is*] undoubtedly greatest task our diplomacy has ever faced and probably greatest it will ever have to face. . . . I would like to record my conviction that problem is within our power to solve—and that without recourse to any general military conflict. And in support of this conviction there are certain observations of a more encouraging nature I should like to make:

(1) Soviet power . . . does not take unnecessary risks. . . . For this reason it can easily withdraw—and usually does—when strong resistance is encountered at any point. Thus, if the adversary has sufficient force and makes clear his readiness to use it, he rarely has to do so. . . .

(2) Gauged against Western World as a whole, Soviets are still by far the weaker force. Thus, their success will really depend on degree of cohesion, firmness and vigor which Western World can muster. . . .

(3) Success of Soviet system, as form of internal power, is not yet finally proven. . . .

(4) All Soviet propaganda beyond Soviet security sphere is basically negative and destructive. It should therefore be relatively easy to combat it by any intelligent and really constructive program.

For these reasons I think we may approach calmly and with good heart problem of how to deal with Russia. . . . [B]y way of conclusion, following comments:

(1) Our first step must be to apprehend, and recognize for what it is, the nature of the movement with which we are dealing. . . .

(2) We must see that our public is educated to realities of Russian situation. . . .

(3) Much depends on health and vigor of our own society. World communism is like malignant parasite which feeds only on diseased tissue. . . .

(4) We must formulate and put forward for other nations a much more positive and constructive picture of sort of world we would like to see than we have put forward in past. . . .

(5)   Finally we must have courage and self-confidence to cling to our own methods and conceptions of human society. After all, the greatest danger that can befall us in coping with this problem of Soviet communism, is that we shall allow ourselves to become like those with whom we are coping.

KENNAN

Wallace Questions Containment

Not all American officials approved of President Truman's policy of firm containment of the Soviet Union. In an address delivered September 12, 1946, in New York City, Secretary of Commerce Henry A. Wallace publicly encouraged Truman to reduce tensions with the Soviets through accommodation and compromise and thereby avoid a catastrophic military conflict. Truman rejected such advice and within weeks of Wallace's address fired him from the cabinet. Selected from Vital Speeches of the Day *12 (October 1, 1946): 738–40.*

Tonight I want to talk about peace—and how to get peace. Never have the common people of all lands so longed for peace. Yet, never in a time of comparative peace have they feared war so much.

Up till now peace has been negative and unexciting. War has been positive and exciting. Far too often, hatred and fear, intolerance and deceit have had the upper hand over love and confidence, trust and joy. Far too often, the law of nations has been the law of the jungle; and the constructive spiritual forces of the Lord have bowed to the destructive forces of Satan.

During the past year or so, the significance of peace has been increased immeasurably by the atom bomb, guided missiles and airplanes which soon will travel as fast as sound. Make no mistake about it—another war would hurt the United States many times as much as the last war. We cannot rest in the assurance that we

---

Excerpt from "The Way to Peace," speech by Henry A. Wallace, as it appeared in *Vital Speeches of the Day*, Vol. XII, No. 24, City News Publishing Company, October 1, 1946.

invented the atom bomb—and therefore that this agent of destruction will work best for us. He who trusts in the atom bomb will sooner or later perish by the atom bomb—or something worse.

I say this as one who steadfastly backed preparedness throughout the Thirties. We have no use for namby-pamby pacifism. But we must realize that modern inventions have now made peace the most exciting thing in the world—and we should be willing to pay a just price for peace. If modern war can cost us $400 billion, we should be willing and happy to pay much more for peace. But certainly, the cost of peace is to be measured not in dollars but in the hearts and minds of men.

The price of peace—for us and for every nation in the world—is the price of giving up prejudice, hatred, fear, and ignorance.

. . . I plead for an America vigorously dedicated to peace—just as I plead for opportunities for the next generation throughout the world to enjoy the abundance which now, more than ever before, is the birthright of man.

To achieve lasting peace, we must study in detail just how the Russian character was formed—by invasions of Tartars, Mongols, Germans, Poles, Swedes, and French; by the czarist rule based on ignorance, fear and force; by the intervention of the British, French and Americans in Russian affairs from 1919 to 1921; by the geography of the huge Russian land mass situated strategically between Europe and Asia; and by the vitality derived from the rich Russian soil and the strenuous Russian climate. Add to all this the tremendous emotional power which Marxism and Leninism gives to the Russian leaders—and then we can realize that we are reckoning with a force which cannot be handled successfully by a "Get tough with Russia" policy. "Getting tough" never bought anything real and lasting—whether for schoolyard bullies or businessmen or world powers. The tougher we get, the tougher the Russians will get.

. . . We most earnestly want peace with Russia—but we want to be met half way. We want cooperation. And I believe that we can get cooperation once Russia understands that our primary objective is neither saving the British Empire nor purchasing oil in the Near East with the lives of American soldiers. . . .

The real peace treaty we now need is between the United States and Russia. On our part, we should recognize that we have no more business in the *political* affairs of Eastern Europe than Russia has in the *political* affairs of Latin America, Western Europe and the United States. . . .

As for Germany, we all must recognize that an equitable settlement, based on a unified German nation, is absolutely essential to any lasting European settlement. This means that Russia must be assured that never again can German industry be converted into military might to be used against her—and Britain, Western Europe and the United States must be certain that Russia's Germany policy will not become a tool of Russian design against Western Europe.

The Russians have no more business in stirring up native communists to political activity in Western Europe, Latin America and the United States than we have in interfering in the politics of Eastern Europe and Russia. We know what Russia is up to in Eastern Europe, for example, and Russia knows what we are up to. We cannot permit the door to be closed against our trade in Eastern Europe any more than we can in China. But at the same time we have to recognize that the Balkans are closer to Russia than to us—and that Russia cannot permit either England or the United States to dominate the politics of that area.

. . . We are still arming to the hilt. Our excessive expenses for military purposes are the chief cause for our unbalanced budget. If taxes are to be lightened we must have the basis of a real peace with Russia—a peace that cannot be broken by extremist propagandists. . . .

Russian ideas of social-economic justice are going to govern nearly a third of the world. Our ideas of free enterprise democracy will govern much of the rest. The two ideas will endeavor to prove which can deliver the most satisfaction to the common man in their respective areas of political dominance. But by mutual agreement, this competition should be put on a friendly basis and the Russians should stop conniving against us in certain areas of the world just as we should stop scheming against them in other parts of the world. Let the results of the two systems speak for themselves.

Meanwhile, the Russians should stop teaching that their form of communism must, by force if necessary, ultimately triumph over democratic capitalism—while we should close our ears to those among us who would have us believe that Russian communism and our free enterprise system cannot live, one with another, in a profitable and productive peace.

Under friendly peaceful competition the Russian world and the American world will gradually become more alike. The Russians will be forced to grant more and more of the personal freedoms; and we shall become more and more absorbed with the problems of social-economic justice.

Russia must be convinced that we are not planning for war against her and we must be certain that Russia is not carrying on territorial expansion or world domination through native communists faithfully following every twist and turn in the Moscow party line. But in this competition, we must insist on an open door for trade throughout the world. There will always be an ideological conflict—but that is no reason why diplomats cannot work out a basis for both systems to live safely in the world side by side.

The Truman Doctrine

President Truman's handling of an early 1947 crisis in Greece reflected his resolve to deal firmly with the Soviet Union. In February 1947, British officials explained to Truman that financial troubles would compel them to suspend their support of the monarchy of Greece, which was resisting an internal revolt by leftists. In a personal appearance at a joint session of Congress on March 12, Truman portrayed the rebellion in Greece as evidence of covert Soviet expansionism and vowed to resist it with massive financial assistance to the government in Athens. He also planned to provide aid to Turkey to encourage it to resist Soviet pressures for territorial and political concessions. Congress endorsed the president's policy, commonly called the Truman Doctrine, by allocating some $400 million in assistance to the two Mediterranean states. Truman's address, excerpted below, appears in Public Papers of the Presidents of the United States: Harry S. Truman, 1947 *(Washington, 1963), 176–80.*

The gravity of the situation which confronts the world today necessitates my appearance before a joint session of the Congress. The foreign policy and the national security of this country are involved. One aspect of the present situation, which I present to you at this time for your consideration and decision, concerns Greece and Turkey.

The United States has received from the Greek Government an urgent appeal for financial and economic assistance. . . . [A]ssistance is imperative if Greece is to survive as a free nation.

I do not believe that the American people and the Congress wish to turn a deaf ear to the appeal of the Greek Government. . . . The very existence of the Greek state is today threatened by the terrorist activities of several thousand armed men, led by Communists, who defy the government's authority at a number of points, particularly along the northern boundaries. . . .

. . . [T]he Greek Government is unable to cope with the situation. The Greek army is small and poorly equipped. It needs supplies

President Harry S. Truman. (Courtesy of The Library of Congress.)

and equipment if it is to restore authority to the government throughout Greek territory. Greece must have assistance if it is to become a self-supporting and self-respecting democracy. The United States must supply this assistance. . . .

Greece's neighbor, Turkey, also deserves our attention. The future of Turkey as an independent and economically sound state is clearly no less important to the freedom-loving peoples of the world than the future of Greece. . . . Turkey now needs our support.

. . . I am fully aware of the broad implications involved if the United States extends assistance to Greece and Turkey, and I shall discuss these implications with you at this time.

One of the primary objectives of the foreign policy of the United States is the creation of conditions in which we and other nations will be able to work out a way of life free from coercion. This was a fundamental issue in the war with Germany and Japan. . . . At the present moment in world history nearly every nation must choose between alternative ways of life. The choice is too often not a free one.

One way of life is based upon the will of the majority, and is distinguished by free institutions, representative government, free elections, guarantees of individual liberty, freedom of speech and religion, and freedom from political oppression.

The second way of life is based upon the will of a minority forcibly imposed upon the majority. It relies upon terror and oppression, a controlled press and radio, fixed elections, and the suppression of personal freedoms.

I believe that it must be the policy of the United States to support free peoples who are resisting attempted subjugation by armed minorities or by outside pressures. I believe that we must assist free peoples to work out their own destinies in their own way. I believe that our help should be primarily through economic and financial aid which is essential to economic stability and orderly political processes.

. . . If Greece should fall under the control of an armed minority, the effect upon its neighbor, Turkey, would be immediate and serious. Confusion and disorder might well spread throughout the entire Middle East. Moreover, the disappearance of Greece as an independent state would have a profound effect upon those countries in Europe whose peoples are struggling against great difficulties to maintain their freedoms and their independence while they repair the damages of war. . . . The seeds of totalitarian regimes are nurtured by misery and want. They spread and grow in the evil soil of poverty and strife. They reach their full growth when the hope of a people for a better life has died.

We must keep that hope alive.

The free peoples of the world look to us for support in maintaining their freedoms. If we falter in our leadership, we may endanger the peace of the world—and we shall surely endanger the welfare of this Nation.

Soviets Denounce the Truman Doctrine

On March 14, 1947, the day after Truman's speech to Congress, the Moscow newspaper Izvestia printed a broadside of the Truman Doctrine that likely reflected official Soviet thinking. The statement suggested that neither Greece nor Turkey was threatened by external forces and that American aid would lead to American domination of both states. Abridged from Izvestia, with English translation provided by Dr. Kurt Schultz of the staff of The Russian Review.

On 12 March, U.S. President H. Truman addressed a message to Congress in which he requested $400 million for urgent aid to Greece and Turkey, and permission to send American civilian and military personnel to these countries and to provide "specially selected" Greek and Turkish personnel with training and instruction by Americans.

To justify his proposal, Truman declared that Greece's economic and political situation was desperate, and that England could no longer take care of the Greeks. "England," said Mr. Truman, "faces the necessity of reducing and liquidating its obligations in several parts of the world, including Greece."

Turkey, for its part, needs America's "immediate assistance." It is true that Turkey, unlike Greece, did not suffer from the Second World War, but she needed England's and America's financial aid, said Truman, "for implementing the modernization necessary to maintain her national integrity." And since the British government, "due to its own difficulties," is in this case not able to extend financial or other assistance to the Turks, then the United States, in Truman's opinion, "must" extend that assistance.

And thus the American Congress is asked to promptly sanction two "good deeds": to save Greece from internal disorders and to pay for the costs of "modernizing" Turkey, upon which, allegedly, her very existence depends.

There can be no doubt that the Tsaldaris administration's tearful pleas to the USA for help is clear evidence of the bankruptcy of Greece's internal political regime, which in Truman's address is portrayed flatteringly. What is key here is not only and not so much the mercenary Greek monarchists and their allies, who are being politely portrayed to American congressmen as the direct descendants of the legendary defender of Thermopylae, Tsar Leonid.

It is well known that the real masters of Greece have been and remain British military authorities. British troops have been on Greek territory since 1944. On Churchill's initiative, England took upon itself the responsibility for "stabilizing" political conditions in Greece. English authorities have not only assisted in perpetuating and nurturing the rule of reactionary and anti-democratic forces in Greece, showing at the same time an extreme indiffer-

---

Excerpted from *Izvestia*, March 14, 1947, translated by Dr. Kurt Schultz.

ence to and even supporting people who actively and consciously cooperated with the Germans. All the political and economic activities of every manner of coalition and short-lived Greek governments have been carried out under close English control and direction.

The result of this is now before us: complete bankruptcy. English troops have not brought peace and tranquillity to a tortured Greece. The Greek people have been cast into the abyss of new sufferings, hunger, and poverty. Instead of subsiding, the civil war is acquiring ever more fierce forms.

Has not the presence of foreign troops on Greek territory actually contributed to this sad situation? Doesn't England, which declared itself to be Greece's guardian, bear the responsibility for its ward's bankruptcy?

The American president's message skirts these perfectly natural questions. The reason for such delicacy is understandable: the United States does not wish to criticize English policy because it intends to follow the English example. No wonder the *Times* of London warmly welcomed Truman's address, while the *Daily Telegraph* noted that his speech "fully justifies English policy in Greece." It is clear from Truman's speech that the United States does not plan to change the course set by British policy in Greece. But in light of this, one cannot expect better results.

The American government has no intention whatsoever of dealing with the Greek question in a fashion that one might expect of a member of the United Nations that is concerned about the fate of another of its members. Clearly no one in Washington wishes to consider the obligations the U.S. government accepted with regard to the UN. Showing unusual nervousness, Truman didn't even consider it necessary to wait for the results of the work of a special commission of the Security Council that had been sent to Greece to investigate the situation on the spot. In vain, the American president remembered that "the United States took upon itself the leading role in creating the United Nations." In any event, it wasn't worth remembering this in order to now declare his desire to act through the head of the United Nations, not taking into account the existence of the international organization and forgetting that in New York there meets a continually active international organ—the Security Council.

Truman has ignored both the international organization as well as the sovereignty of Greece. Indeed, what will remain of

Greek sovereignty when "American military and civilian personnel" are sitting on the head of the Greek government and when these "personnel" begin to run the show with the help of their 250 million American dollars? The sovereignty and independence of Greece above all else will be the victims of such peculiar "defense." The Greek people, who have been engaged in a heroic struggle for their independence and freedom, do not deserve this sort of attention. If this is what Messrs. Tsaldarises aim for, then so much the worse for them, since they're the ones who have led Greece into this situation.

The ever-suffering Greek people are now threatened with the replacement of one "master"—England—with another "master"—the United States of America. It is impossible to conceal American pretensions to American predominance in Greece by justifying those pretensions as defense of the freedom and independence of the Greek people.

American arguments for assisting Turkey are based on the existence of a threat to the integrity of Turkish territory, even though no one or nothing is threatening Turkey's integrity.

American "aid" to Turkey is clearly directed toward subordinating that country as well to U.S. control, after which point it will be impossible even to talk about independent domestic and foreign Turkish policy, since that policy will be under the control of American imperialism. Some American commentators are openly speaking of this. Walter Lippmann frankly points out in the *New York Herald Tribune* that the American "alliance with Turkey" would give the United States a "strategic position that is incomparably more favorable than any other from which to exercise authority in the Middle East." And the *New York Times*, commenting upon Truman's message to Congress, bombastically proclaims the advent of "the age of American responsibility."

But, the question arises, what else is this monopolistic "American responsibility" but a screen for expansionist plans?

Arguments that the U.S.A. "is obliged to save" Greece and Turkey from the expansion of so-called "totalitarian states" is not new. Hitler also relied on the Bolsheviks when he wanted to pave the way for his conquests. Now they want to subordinate Greece and Turkey, and they are trying to conceal their expansionist plans by raising a racket about "totalitarian states." This is even more attractive given that the United States is elbowing non-totalitarian Britain out of yet another one or two countries.

Mr. Truman's address could not help but attract the attention of the broad public in both the U.S.A. and abroad. One cannot say that it has not met serious criticism even within the circles of the U.S. Congress. A group of 13 American congressmen tried to talk Truman out of making the address before he delivered it. As the Democratic Senator Taylor declared, "We would be disgusted by a proposal to vote for rendering financial aid to a monarchist government that is persecuting those who fought against the Nazis."

Another Democratic Senator, Johnson, expressed the same thought: "I wholeheartedly sympathize with giving food as aid, without political aims, but the president made no distinction between food and bullets, and that is the reason for my disappointment. I am not sympathetic to the dispatch of our military personnel to Greece and Turkey even as advisers. Military aid to Turkey and Greece could lead to military intervention in other parts of the world. I am ready to give millions in support of aid to hungry people, but not one cent for helping rotting monarchies."

The Democratic Senator Pepper declared that "Truman's recommendation, made without any consultation with the United Nations, constitutes a threat to the UN and lays unknown obligations upon the United States." Also characteristic was the observation of the chairman of the House of Representatives' Budget Committee, the Republican Knudson, who said that "the supporters of Truman's program apparently will not be satisfied until the United States goes bankrupt." Henry Wallace came out with a sharply negative judgment of Truman's address, as did several other leading American figures.

Before us is yet another intrusion by the United States into the affairs of another state. The pretensions of the United States to leadership in international affairs are growing along with the appetite of the interested American circles. But American leaders, operating in new historical circumstances, are not taking into account that the old methods of colonizers and hard-headed politicians have outlived their age and are doomed to failure.

This is the main weakness of Mr. Truman's address.

NSC-68 and the Enduring Cold War

American-Soviet tensions provoked by the Truman Doctrine were exacerbated in 1948-49 by such other Western initiatives as the Marshall Plan, the North Atlantic Treaty Organization, and by the communist coup d'etat in Czechoslovakia and the Soviet blockade of Berlin. In 1949, when Communists seized power in China after a long civil war and when the Soviets successfully tested an atomic device years before Western experts anticipated they would, American concerns escalated sharply. U.S. officials conducted a major re-examination of foreign policy and produced a top secret planning document called NSC-68. The document attributed to Moscow a concerted plan of global conquest and proposed a massive increase in U.S. defense preparations to deter Soviet aggression and thereby create opportunities to weaken the Soviet Union through political and economic means. Drafted in April 1950, NSC-68 was approved by President Truman as an official policy document after the outbreak of the Korean War in June. Excerpted from U.S. Department of State, Foreign Relations of the United States, 1950 *(Washington, 1977), 1:237–38, 240–41, 243–44, 263, 272, 282, 285–87, 292.*

During the span of one generation, the international distribution of power has been fundamentally altered. For several centuries it had proved impossible for any one nation to gain such preponderant strength that a coalition of other nations could not in time face it with greater strength. The international scene was marked by recurring periods of violence and war, but a system of sovereign and independent states was maintained, over which no state was able to achieve hegemony.

Two complex sets of factors have now basically altered this historical distribution of power. First, the defeat of Germany and Japan and the decline of the British and French Empires have interacted with the development of the United States and the Soviet Union in such a way that power has increasingly gravitated to these two centers. Second, the Soviet Union, unlike previous aspirants to hegemony, is animated by a new fanatic faith, antithetical to our own, and seeks to impose its absolute authority over the rest of the world. . . .

. . . [A]ny substantial further extension of the area under the domination of the Kremlin would raise the possibility that no coalition adequate to confront the Kremlin with greater strength could be assembled. It is in this context that this Republic and its citizens in the ascendancy of their strength stand in their deepest peril.

The issues that face us are momentous, involving the fulfillment or destruction not only of this Republic but of civilization itself. . . . The fundamental purpose of the United States . . . is to assure the integrity and vitality of our free society, which is founded upon the dignity and worth of the individual. . . . The fundamental design of those who control the Soviet Union and the international communist movement is to retain and solidify their absolute power, first in the Soviet Union and second in the areas now under their control. In the minds of the Soviet leaders, however, achievement of this design requires the dynamic extension of their authority and the ultimate elimination of any effective opposition to their authority. . . . Thus unwillingly our free society finds itself mortally challenged by the Soviet system. No other value system is so wholly irreconcilable with ours, so implacable in its purpose to destroy ours, so capable of turning to its own uses the most dangerous and divisive trends in our own society, no other so skillfully and powerfully evokes the elements of irrationality in human nature everywhere, and no other has the support of a great and growing center of military power. . . .

In a shrinking world, which now faces the threat of atomic warfare, it is not an adequate objective merely to seek to check the Kremlin design, for the absence of order among nations is becoming less and less tolerable. This fact imposes on us, in our own interests, the responsibility of world leadership. . . .

The Kremlin is able to select whatever means are expedient in seeking to carry out its fundamental design. . . . We have no such freedom of choice, and least of all in the use of force. Resort to war is not only a last resort for a free society, but it is also an act which cannot definitively end the fundamental conflict in the realm of ideas. . . .

Practical and ideological considerations therefore both impel us to the conclusion that we have no choice but to demonstrate the superiority of the idea of freedom by its constructive application, and to attempt to change the world situation by means short of war in such a way as to frustrate the Kremlin design and hasten the decay of the Soviet system.

. . . It is quite clear from Soviet theory and practice that the Kremlin seeks to bring the free world under its dominion by the methods of the cold war. . . .

Four possible courses of action by the United States in the present situation can be distinguished. They are:

a. Continuation of current policies . . . ;

b. Isolation;

c. War; and

d. A more rapid building up of the political, economic, and military strength of the free world than provided under *a*, with the purpose of reaching, if possible, a tolerable state of order among nations without war and of preparing to defend ourselves in the event that the free world is attacked.

. . . [Choice D] is the only course which is consistent with progress toward achieving our fundamental purpose. . . . It is necessary to have the military power to deter, if possible, Soviet expansion, and to defeat, if necessary, aggressive Soviet or Soviet-directed actions of a limited or total character. . . .

A program for rapidly building up strength and improving political and economic conditions will place heavy demands on our courage and intelligence; it will be costly; it will be dangerous. But half-measures will be more costly and more dangerous, for they will be inadequate to prevent and may actually invite war. Budgetary considerations will need to be subordinated to the stark fact that our very independence as a nation may be at stake.

A comprehensive and decisive program . . . would probably involve:

(1) The development of an adequate political and economic framework for the achievement of our long-range objectives.

(2) A substantial increase in expenditures for military purposes. . . .

(3) A substantial increase in military assistance programs, designed to foster cooperative efforts, which will adequately and efficiently meet the requirements of our allies. . . .

(4) Some increase in economic assistance programs and recognition of the need to continue these programs until their purposes have been accomplished.

(5) A concerted attack on the problem of the United States balance of payments. . . .

(6) Development of programs designed to build and maintain confidence among other peoples in our strength and resolution, and to wage overt psychological warfare calculated to encourage mass defections from Soviet allegiance and to frustrate the Kremlin design in other ways.

(7) Intensification of affirmative and timely measures and operations by covert means in the fields of economic warfare and political and psychological warfare with a view to fomenting and supporting unrest and revolt in selected strategic satellite countries.

(8) Development of internal security and civilian defense programs.

(9) Improvement and intensification of intelligence activities.

(10) Reduction of Federal expenditures for purposes other than defense and foreign assistance, if necessary by the deferment of certain desirable programs.

(11) Increased taxes.

... The Soviet Union is currently devoting about 40 percent of available resources ... to military expenditures. ... In an emergency the Soviet Union could increase the allocation of resources to these purposes to about 50 percent, or by one-fourth.

The United States is currently devoting about 22 percent of its gross national product ... to military expenditures. ... In an emergency the United States could devote upward of 50 percent of its gross national product to these purposes (as it did during the last war), an increase of several times present expenditures for direct and indirect military purposes and foreign assistance. ...

The threat to the free world involved in the development of the Soviet Union's atomic and other capabilities will rise steadily and rather rapidly. For the time being, the United States possesses a marked atomic superiority over the Soviet Union which ... inhibits aggressive Soviet action. This provides an opportunity for the United States, in cooperation with other free countries, to launch a build-up of strength which will support a firm policy directed to the frustration of the Kremlin design. ...

The whole success of the proposed program hangs ultimately on recognition by this Government, the American people, and all free peoples, that the cold war is in fact a real war in which the survival of the free world is at stake. ... The prosecution of the program will require of us all the ingenuity, sacrifice, and unity demanded by the vital importance of the issue and the tenacity to persevere until our national objectives have been attained.

Questions

---

1. *What was the fundamental nature of American-Soviet conflict in the late 1940s? How extensively did the worldviews of the two powers differ?*
2. *Was the Truman Doctrine an American effort to preserve the independence of Greece and Turkey, or an American quest to gain dominance over both countries?*
3. *Were the policy prescriptions in NSC-68 valid, in your judgment, on the basis of circumstances facing the United States in 1950?*
4. *On the basis of these documents, which power do you think was most accountable for the Cold War?*

FURTHER READING

Traditional histories of the early Cold War include Herbert Feis, From Trust to Terror: The Onset of the Cold War, 1945–1950 *(New York, 1970); Hugh Thomas,* Armed Truce: The Beginnings of the Cold War, 1945–1946 *(New York, 1987); and Randall B. Woods and Howard Jones,* Dawning of the Cold War: The United States, Quest for Order *(Athens, Georgia, 1991). For revisionist accounts, see Gar Alperovitz,* Atomic Diplomacy: Hiroshima and Potsdam *(New York, 1965); Lloyd C. Gardner,* Architects of Illusion: Men and Ideas in American Foreign Policy, 1941–1949 *(Chicago, 1970); Thomas G. Paterson,* Soviet-American Confrontation: Postwar Reconstruction and the Origins of the Cold War *(Baltimore, 1973); and Joyce and Gabriel Kolko,* The Limits of Power: The World and United States Foreign Policy, 1945–1954 *(New York, 1972). Post-revisionist and synthetic works are Melvyn P. Leffler,* A Preponderance of Power: National Security, the Truman Administration, and the Cold War *(Stanford, 1992); James Gormly,* The Collapse of the Grand Alliance, 1945–1948 *(Baton Rouge, 1987); and John Lewis Gaddis,* The United States and the Origins of the Cold War, 1941–1947 *(New York, 1972). On specific aspects of U.S. policy, see Bruce Cumings,* The Origins of the Korean War, *vol. 2:* The Roaring of the Cataract, 1947–1950 *(Princeton, 1990); Michael J. Hogan,* The Marshall Plan: America, Britain, and the Reconstruction of Western Europe, 1947–1952 *(New York, 1987); and Lawrence Kaplan,* The United States and NATO: The Formative Years *(Lexington, Kentucky, 1984).*

American Life
in the 1950s

David L. Stebenne

INTRODUCTION

Understanding the period in American history that we call the fifties poses a major challenge for students of the nation's past. In part that is because the fifties is still recent enough that there are many Americans alive today who experienced it firsthand. The tendency in such circumstances is to generalize from one's own experience, which can lead to a distorted, or at least incomplete, understanding of the past. The closeness of the 1950s to the present also complicates our efforts to understand it in another way. During the 1950s, American life first assumed a shape that is familiar to most Americans even today. In a very real sense, the 1950s was the beginning of life in our own time. For that reason, achieving a sense of historical perspective on the fifties is harder than it is for earlier periods in American history.

There are other obstacles to obtaining a clear understanding of what life in the 1950s was like. One has to do with the process of social change that began in the early 1960s and continued for the next three decades. Many of the reforms that began in the 1960s were intended by their creators to address what they saw as the least attractive aspects of life in the fifties. One result has been to emphasize in history texts, movies, and popular culture more generally the shortcomings of American society during that time. What has been obscured in the process is a more complete and balanced picture of life in the 1950s. The period's complex, even contradictory, character has also made the task of understanding it difficult. Although a time of great international tensions and fear of nuclear war, many Americans during the 1950s enjoyed more security, economic and psychological, than they have since. A period of anti-radical hysteria, the fifties was also one in which support for the welfare state, high and progressive taxation, and labor unions was much greater than today. While an enormous increase in child-bearing, the so-called "baby boom," took place during the 1950s, at that same time married women streamed into the paid labor force in unprecedented numbers. One could find many more examples to illustrate the same basic point.

A final source of difficulty in understanding the 1950s has to do with periodization. We often tend to think of decades as having their own special character, but rarely does a major historical event or phenomenon fit neatly into a single decade. For example, we tend to think of the Great Depression as having taken place during "the thirties," but it actually began in the late 1920s and lasted into the early 1940s. The 1950s was a similarly "long" decade, one that began in the winter of 1948 and stretched on into the spring of 1963. When Americans talk about what was distinctive about life in "the fifties," they usually are referring to events that took place during that larger period of time.

The obstacles to understanding what American life in the 1950s was really like loom large for students of American history. Yet, that basic question remains: what was "the fifties" about? More specifically, what were the distinctive features of life during that time, and how did they relate to one another?

SOME ASPECTS OF THE '50S SYSTEM

There were, of course, many aspects of American life during the 1950s, some that stemmed directly from the economic boom, and others whose relationship to it seems much more attenuated and uncertain. The following readings provide insight into several of the most important aspects, from the perspectives of those who lived during that time. Given how many aspects of life in the fifties there were to choose from, including all of them here is not possible. For example, such topics as the religious revival of the 1950s and the labor movement, both of which were major social forces during that time, are not dealt with below. Despite these omissions, the passages that follow offer insight into what life was like during the 1950s, and into how economic conditions combined with other factors to create a distinctive social system.

The Anti-Radical Hysteria Hits Hollywood

In the late 1940s, a fear of radicals and especially Communists emerged in the United States. Encouraged by some influential politicians, most notably Senator Joseph McCarthy of Wisconsin, and by congressional investigating committees, that fear soon developed into a full-blown hysteria, one that today is known as McCarthyism. Although the U.S. Senate condemned McCarthy in 1954 for his irresponsible accusations, the climate of fear persisted throughout the remainder of the 1950s. Among the groups directly affected by the hysteria was the movie industry. In a 1948 piece for The New Yorker magazine, writer Lillian Ross described the hysteria's initial impact on Hollywood. Abridged from "Onward and Upward with the Arts," The New Yorker, *February 21, 1948, 42, 44, 46.*

The House Un-American Activities Committee (HUAC) begins its investigation of communists in Hollywood, 1947. (Courtesy of Corbis-Bettmann.)

A FEW weeks ago, many people in Hollywood received through the mails a booklet called "Screen Guide for Americans," published by the Motion Picture Alliance for the Preservation of American Ideals and containing a list of "Do"s and "Don't"s. "This is the raw iron from which a new curtain around Hollywood will be fashioned," one man assured me solemnly. "This is the first step—not to fire people, not to get publicity, not to clean Communism out of motion pictures but to rigidly control all the contents of all pictures for Right Wing political purposes." The Motion Picture Association of America has not yet publicly adopted the "Screen Guide for Americans" in place of its own "A Code to Govern the Making of Motion and Talking Pictures," which advances such tenets as "The just rights, history, and feelings of any nation are entitled to consideration and respectful treatment" and "The treatment of bedrooms must be governed by

Excerpts from "Come In, Lassie!" by Lillian Ross, reprinted from the *The New Yorker*, Vol. 23, No. 53, February 21, 1948. Reprinted by permission; Copyright © 1948, 1976 The New Yorker Magazine, Inc. All rights reserved.

good taste and delicacy." Although it is by no means certain that the industry has got around to following these old rules, either to the letter or in the spirit, there is a suspicion that it may have already begun at least to paraphrase some of the "Screen Guide's" pronouncements, which appear under such headings as "Don't Smear the Free Enterprise System," "Don't Deify the 'Common Man,'" "Don't Glorify the Collective," "Don't Glorify Failure," "Don't Smear Success," and "Don't Smear Industrialists." "All too often, industrialists, bankers, and businessmen are presented on the screen as villains, crooks, chiselers, or exploiters," the "Guide" observes. "It is the *moral* (no, not just political but *moral*) duty of every decent man in the motion picture industry to throw into the ashcan, where it belongs, every story that smears industrialists as such." Another admonition reads, "Don't give to your characters—as a sign of villainy, as a damning characteristic—a desire to make money." And another, "Don't permit any disparagement or defamation of personal success. It is the Communists' intention to make people think that personal success is somehow achieved at the expense of others and that every successful man has hurt somebody by becoming successful." The booklet warns, "Don't tell people that man is a helpless, twisted, drooling, sniveling, neurotic weakling. Show the world an *American* kind of man, for a change." The "Guide" instructs people in the industry, "Don't let yourself be fooled when the Reds tell you that what they want to destroy are men like Hitler and Mussolini. What they want to destroy are men like Shakespeare, Chopin, and Edison." Still another of the "Don't"s says, "Don't ever use any lines about 'the common man' or 'the little people.' It is not the American idea to be either 'common' or 'little.'" . . .

I was given a copy of "Screen Guide for Americans" by Mrs. Lela Rogers, one of the founders of the Motion Picture Alliance for the Preservation of American Ideals. Mrs. Rogers, the mother of Ginger, is a pretty, blond-haired lady with a vibrant, birdlike manner. "A lot of people who work in pictures wouldn't know Communism if they saw it," she said to me. "You think that a Communist is a man with a bushy beard. He's not. He's an American, and he's pretty, too." The Congressional investigation of Hollywood, Mrs. Rogers thinks, will result in better pictures and the victory of the Republican Party in the next election [1948]. "Last month, I spoke about Communism at a ten-dollar-a-plate dinner given by the Republican Party," she said. "My goodness, I amassed a lot of money for the campaign. Now I have more speaking engagements than I can possibly fulfill." Mrs. Rogers is also writing screen plays. I wanted to know if she was following the "Do"s and "Don't"s of the "Screen Guide for Americans." "You just bet I am," she said. "My friend Ayn Rand wrote it, and sticking to it is easy as pie. I've just finished a shooting script about a man who learns how to live after he is dead."

Other people in the industry admit that they are following the "Guide" in scripts about the living. One man who is doing that assured me that he nevertheless doesn't need it, that it offers him nothing he didn't already know. "This is new only to the young-sters out here," he said. "They haven't had their profound inten-tions knocked out of them yet, or else they're still earning under five hundred a week. As soon as you become adjusted in this business, you don't need the 'Screen Guide' to tell you what to do." A studio executive in charge of reading scripts believes that Hollywood has a new kind of self-censorship. "It's automatic, like shifting gears," he explained. "I now read scripts through the eyes of the D.A.R., whereas formerly I read them through the eyes of my boss. Why, I suddenly find myself beating my breast and proclaiming my patriotism and exclaiming that I love my wife and kids, of which I have four, with a fifth on the way. I'm all loused up. I'm scared to death, and nobody can tell me it isn't because I'm afraid of being investigated."

The New Suburbia

During the 1950s, suburbs first emerged as a conventional mode of residence for middle-income Americans, many of whom moved to them from central cities. The following passage offers journalist Ralph Martin's view of what life was like in a "typical" new suburb located thirty miles east of New York City. Abridged from Ralph G. Martin, "Life in the New Suburbia," The New York Times Magazine, *January 15, 1950, 40–41.*

THE Howard Handlers have lived here only since September, but when Howard talks about his neighbors—welding boss John Phillips, city fireman Tom Carney and air-conditioning expert Dick Hollis—you'd think he was talking about his closest kin.

"Phillips' wife had a birthday last night and what a time we all had," Howard said. "Hollis brought over his kid and put him in the same bed with the Phillips' two kids and then he took out his guitar and played and played and we just sang all night long.

"I tell ya, the four of us really have it worked out. When the girls go to a garden club meeting, we boys get together and baby-sit and play pinochle. Or one night, we'll all go bowling down at the Village Green. And now we're all taking some of these adult education courses down at the school one night a week. Dick and I are taking a course in 'How to Finish Your Attic' and John's learning photography."

He told how they shared everything they learned: the best stuff to clean tile floors, the cheapest insurance for their thermopane windows, that there was a small ventilator opening that should be screened to keep out field mice. When Howard brought back fresh flowers from his mother, all four homes got some. Each woman already had spliced a piece of her potted plant to give to the others. They even compared electric bills, to see if any one bill was out of line.

"See that door windbreaker," said Howard proudly. "It got loose, so Hollis made angle irons for all four of us. And when I wanted to buy a garbage can, he wouldn't let me. He made me that one out of a fifty-pound grease drum. Now isn't that a beautiful garbage can?"

. . . For newcomers it sometimes becomes overwhelming. You come home from work to find your neighbor (whom you hadn't yet met) had put your milk in her refrigerator so the sun wouldn't spoil it. If you don't have a car, neighbors with cars are always asking your wife, "I'm going shopping. Do you want to come along?"

Before you can ask somebody for the neighbor's lawnmower, he usually volunteers it. One woman left her faucet running and came back to a flooded kitchen, but six neighbors were already mopping it up. If your car gets stuck here, don't worry, the next car that comes along will stop to help. When polio victim Norman Modell came out of the hospital, and needed some strong arms to support him while he tried to walk again, he had all the volunteers he needed.

Perhaps all this explains why Mrs. Edwin Niles said, "For the first time since I left Fordyce, Ark., I really feel at home."

There's a small-town friendliness at the Village Greens (there are three so far, more coming up fast). Modernly styled, the Green is the shopping center for each area—and something more. People are always stopping to talk to each other there. Nobody rushes.

This is a paradise for children. "There are so many babies here that you would think everybody would be blasé about them," said Mrs. Alice Miller. "Still, when a new one is coming, all the neighbors make a fuss over you. I had to go to the hospital soon after I moved in, and neighbors I hadn't even met yet just came in and took over. They pack your bags, drive you to the hospital if your husband's working, take care of your other baby if you have one. And they wouldn't let me buy anything for it either. Tha [that] carriage isn't mine and neither is the crib, and my other neighbor said we could have those baby scales as long as we need them. Somebody here always has a baby a year older."

The slightly older ones never had it so good. If they leave their toys on the walk sometimes, or if they overrun into somebody's

An early and influential postwar suburb: Levittown, New York, during the 1950s. (Courtesy of The National Archives.)

back yard—there's a deep, patient understanding by the neighbors, because they probably also have a child. Children have space to run in, grass to roll in, wading pools, playgrounds. Mothers don't worry too much about cars, because there's almost no transient traffic. People who drive here live here. They don't have to be told to watch out for children—they have their own. And the short, curved streets slow down the strangers.

When you talk to the pediatricians (there are six here now, more due any minute), they tell you how much better physically children are here, compared to city kids. But that's a thing you see for yourself. If that was the only reason for moving out here, it would be reason enough for most families.

The Military Experience in Korea

Military service was a common experience for American men during the 1950s, thanks to a peacetime draft and especially the Korean War, which lasted from 1950 to 1953. In the following passage, Korean War veteran Ed Simmons captures the nature of that experience with his description of the American amphibious landing at Inchon in September 1950, a key turning point in the conflict. Abridged from Rudy Tomedi, No Bugles, No Drums: An Oral History of the Korean War *(New York, 1993), 31–34.*

The whole thing looked like an invitation to disaster. I didn't know it at the time, but the leadership of the Marine Corps had great reservations about it. The navy flat out didn't want to do it. But MacArthur had brought everyone around. His personal powers of persuasion were incredible. And of course his confidence knew no bounds. There was that famous meeting held on the twenty-third of August in Tokyo, with all the top military people, that ended with MacArthur going to the map and saying, "We will land at Inchon, and I will crush them."

Our regimental commander was the legendary Lewis B. Puller, probably the most battle-scarred and decorated marine in the history of the Corps. And after we'd listened with the gravest of reservations to the briefing, Chesty Puller got up and gave one of his famous inspirational speeches. It went about like this: "I don't give a blank how many blankety-blank Koreans are defending the blankety-blank beach. We'll find out what's on the beach when we get there. And as far as you people are concerned, I had to wait twenty years between wars, while you get one every five years. You've been willing to live by the sword, and you'd damn well better be willing to die by the sword."

With that reverberating in our heads, we were sent out to start loading for Inchon. . . .

The invasion started on the morning of September 15 with the assault on Wolmi-do, a fortified island just outside the harbor. Wolmi-do had to be taken first, and the plan was to take it on the morning tide with one battalion of marines, who would then hold it until the rest of the invasion force came in on the evening tide to take Inchon itself, one segment landing on Red Beach and the other on Blue Beach.

The two beaches were four miles apart, at opposite ends of the city. I was assigned to Blue Beach and I was on the bridge of our LST [large ship used for amphibious operations] for most of the day, listening to what I could of the radio traffic, and trying to see what I could. It was a misty day with light rain, and with the smoke of the naval gunfire and the burning city, it made for a very heavy smog over the landing area.

Wolmi-do was taken on schedule. The morning tide went out, and as we waited for the evening tide the navy continued to fire on Inchon. The Corsairs flew in all day strafing and bombing. One of the most awesome sights was the rocket ships, the "floating shotguns" as they were called. Within a space of about ten minutes one of these ships could release a thousand rockets, and I remember how they would go off with a terrific whoosh, practically all at once, and streak off into the gloom with fiery red tails.

At about three in the afternoon we loaded into our amtracs [amphibious tractor], and when we pulled away from the LST the first thing I looked for was a guide boat. These were vessels equipped with radios and various other gear to keep the landing boats from getting lost.

U.S. troops fighting in Korea, February 1951. (U.S. Army Photo.)

When we found one I went up onto the bridge and asked for directions to Blue Beach Two. A semi-hysterical ensign pointed to where the smoke was the thickest and said, "That way, I think."

So we started off in that direction, and presently an LCVP [landing craft] came alongside my amtrac. I thought that was our wave guide, but it turned out to be a boatload of Koreans who were being parceled out as interpreters.

Two of these Koreans tumbled into my boat. Well, whatever language they knew, English wasn't one of them. We couldn't make ourselves understood.

I had a map, and finally I decided I'd have to figure things out for myself. But I didn't have a compass, so I asked the amtrac driver if there was one in the amtrac.

He looked at his instrument panel and shrugged. "Search me," he said. "Six weeks ago I was driving a truck in San Francisco."

That's generally the way things went. It was a scene of almost total chaos. Various waves of the invasion force were wandering around in confusion, trying to find their way to the beaches through this immense pall of smoke. And by this time it was also

143

getting dark. There were nowhere near the number of guide boats there should have been. I've said many times that if those beaches had been defended by Germans or Japanese of World War Two caliber, we would not have gotten ashore at Inchon. But they were defended by second-rate troops. And not very many of them.

We finally did manage to find our sector and get ashore. What the boats in the first wave did was come in against the seawall, throw ladders against the wall, and it was up and over the ladders as other marines in the boats lobbed grenades over the wall. But by the time I landed there were big holes in the wall, and we went through one of those.

In front of us there was an open stretch of about a hundred yards, well pockmarked by shell craters, and then some partially destroyed warehouses. Occasionally bullets whined by, but there wasn't a lot of enemy fire, and we were able to move quickly to our assigned positions just outside the town.

Once we secured the beachhead the army's 7th Division, which was landing behind us, was to move through us and continue the advance. This is the way we understood it at the time. What actually happened was that the 7th Division landed behind us and then wheeled south to link up with the Eighth Army, which was hopefully breaking out of the Pusan perimeter, leaving it up to the marines to capture Seoul.

It was about twenty-five miles from Inchon to Seoul. The road was narrow, hard-surfaced, and paralleled by a railway. That road became the axis of our advance, and we moved forward in school-solution manner, in a series of well-coordinated attacks, capturing successive pieces of high ground. There was excellent support by marine air. The landing itself may have been confused, but not the advance on Seoul.

Segregation's Human Cost

Racial segregation or "Jim Crow," as it was more commonly known, was another aspect of American life throughout the 1950s. During that time, social scientists devoted a good deal of effort to studying its effects on members of racial minority groups, especially the children within them.

Many of these studies were summarized in an appendix to the National Association for the Advancement of Colored People's (NAACP) brief in the landmark school desegregation case, Brown v. Board of Education of Topeka, Kansas. *Abridged from Kenneth B. Clark,* Prejudice and Your Child *(Boston, 1955), 168–70.*

At the recent Mid-century White House Conference on Children and Youth, a fact-finding report on the effects of prejudice, discrimination and segregation on the personality development of children was prepared as a basis for some of the deliberations. This report brought together the available social science and psychological studies which were related to the problem of how racial and religious prejudices influenced the development of a healthy personality. . . .

The report indicates that as minority group children learn the inferior status to which they are assigned—as they observe the fact that they are almost always segregated and kept apart from others who are treated with more respect by the society as a whole—they often react with feelings of inferiority and a sense of personal humiliation. Many of them become confused about their own personal worth. On the one hand, like all other human beings they require a sense of personal dignity; on the other hand, almost nowhere in the larger society do they find their own dignity as human beings respected by others. Under these conditions, the minority group child is thrown into a conflict with regard to his feelings about himself and his group. He wonders whether his group and he himself are worthy of no more respect than they receive. This conflict and confusion leads to self-hatred and rejection of his own group.

The report goes on to point out that these children must find ways with which to cope with this conflict. Not every child, of course, reacts with the same patterns of behavior. The particular pattern depends upon many interrelated factors, among which are: the stability and quality of his family relations; the social and economic class to which he belongs; the cultural and educational background of his parents; the particular minority group to which he belongs; his personal characteristics, intelligence, special talents, and personality pattern.

Some children, usually of the lower socio-economic classes, may react by overt aggressions and hostility directed toward their own group or members of the dominant group. Anti-social and delinquent behavior may often be interpreted as reactions to these racial frustrations. These reactions are self-destructive in that the larger society not only punishes those who commit them, but often interprets such aggressive and anti-social behavior as justification for continuing prejudice and segregation.

Middle class and upper class minority group children are likely to react to their racial frustrations and conflicts by withdrawal and submissive behavior. Or, they may react with compensatory and rigid conformity to the prevailing middle class values and standards and an aggressive determination to succeed in these terms in spite of the handicap of their minority status.

The report indicates that minority group children of all social and economic classes often react with a generally defeatist attitude and a lowering of personal ambitions. This, for example, is reflected in a lowering of pupil morale and a depression of the educational aspiration level among minority group children in segregated schools. In producing such effects, segregated schools impair the ability of the child to profit from the educational opportunities provided him.

African American children attend a segregated elementary school. (Courtesy of NAACP.)

Many minority group children of all classes also tend to be hypersensitive and anxious about their relations with the larger society. They tend to see hostility and rejection even in those areas where these might not actually exist.

The report concludes that while the range of individual differences among members of a rejected minority group is as wide as among other peoples, the evidence suggests that all of these children are unnecessarily encumbered in some ways by segregation and its concomitants.

Women and Work

One of the most enduring stereotypes associated with the 1950s is that of married women staying at home rather than holding paying jobs. But as Fortune magazine's labor columnist Daniel Bell pointed out in the middle of the decade, married women then were moving into paying jobs at an unprecedented rate. Abridged from Daniel Bell, "The Great Back-to-Work Movement," Fortune, 54 (July 1956): 91, 93.

Only yesterday, historically speaking, when a girl married she left work, amid envious farewells of her office or shop mates. Today, a girl who announces that she is being married is asked by her supervisor, "Are you taking a trip, or will you be back on Monday?" Whichever the answer, it is becoming increasingly rare that she does not return at all. The figures bearing this out are emphatic. In 1890 a niggling 4 per cent of the country's married women were in the work force; in 1940 there were only 15 per cent; but by April, 1956, 30 per cent of married women held jobs. This development has been recent and swift. During War World II [WW II] the number of married women at work had barely surpassed the number of single girls who held jobs. By 1955, working wives outnumbered the bachelor girls more than two to one.

The striking increase in the number of married women at work resolves one part of the paradox, but there remains the

---

puzzle that the rise occurred during the unexpected boom in babies. Here, too, the American female seems to be showing a new capacity, for more women with small children are at work than ever before. True, the number is still small, but the rate of increase is astonishing. In 1940 only 7 per cent of mothers with children under five held jobs; by 1955 the number had jumped to 18.2 per cent. From any point of view, this development is striking. In 1955 there were 2,500,000 mothers with small children at work; since 1948, a "normal" point because it falls between World War II and Korea, the number had risen 66 per cent.

While such a growth rate is itself a social change of enormous magnitude, it still fails to round out the rise of seven million women in the labor force. Where did the additional millions come from? The answer is: from the ranks of older married women. The middle-aged matron no longer wants to stay at home and be a housewife; she too has joined the 9:00 A.M. to 5:00 P.M. parade. . . .

The most dramatic shift . . . is in the forty-five to fifty-four-year group. Whereas in 1920 fewer than 20 per cent of those women held jobs, today almost 45 per cent are at work, and the proportion is rising. Equally striking is the virtual doubling of the percentage of women between thirty-five and forty-four at work in the last thirty-five years.

This re-entry of the older woman into the labor force creates a new pattern in the life cycle of American women. In the late teens and early twenties, a large number go to work; the number declines during the child-bearing period, then picks up as the children grow older, go to school, and leave home. Re-entry has posed some new problems for the American woman. She has to plan for a "second working life" and for a longer period of employment, and these considerations become increasingly important in her job training and education.

Who works, and why

What has brought the married woman out of the home and into the labor market in such multitudes? . . . There are several elements responsible for this emerging pattern of the behavior of women, especially married women, in the labor force. There is the large number of job opportunities that an expanding economy now offers. There is the free time made available by modern household facilities (e.g., ready-cooked meals). Education, now universal, gives many women a vocational urge that homemaking alone cannot satisfy. A job provides stimulus and companionship that the home in daytime does not. (Typical comment of a working wife: "Now I have something to talk about with my husband when we both come home.") But most significant, perhaps, is the hunger for the appurtenances of a good life that multiple incomes can bring more quickly; the American standard of living has become a built-in automatic "drive" on the part of the American wife. This asserts itself in her reasons for working. It also has affected broad sectors of the U.S. economy.

The social revolution at the turn of the century, which brought the young single woman into the office, created a host of new industries. The young single female, with an income of her own for the first time, splurged wholesale for clothes, beauty aids, entertainment. This new spending produced the fashion industry, the mass production of dresses and coats, the beauty shop and the permanent wave, the silk stockings, and the women's magazines. The Twenties was a gaudy reflection of these hungers. It was a revolution in style. Today new impulses are at work. The married woman at work today (interviewed by FORTUNE in thirty-six cities) wants a house, the durable consumer goods that go with it, and savings to send the children through college. These new, sober impulses are heavily responsible for the enormous boom in consumer durables that underlies the prosperity surge of the last decade. This is the economic consequence of the new role of the woman at work.

. . . Time was, though few are left to recall, when man could still find a world untrammeled by females at some place of employment. Today, "no job is an island." Females are now to be found in such unlikely jobs as railroad trainmen, baggage handlers, furnace tenders, glaziers, auctioneers, plumbers, and jumper men (i.e., connecting cable terminals) in the telephone field. In 1950, for the first time in U.S. history, there was not one category in the published census of occupations that did not have at least a few females.

But while versatile women have poked into every job nook and cranny, the overwhelming number have gone into the traditional female employments. . . . Of the seven million new women in the labor force since 1940, over 40 per cent took clerical jobs. In the factories, great increases were registered in electronics and electrical manufacturing.

An Endangered Environment

During the 1950s, the use of pesticides such as DDT to fight pests became widespread. Although effective in increasing crop yields and in retarding such blights as Dutch elm disease, pesticides also had other, more disturbing, consequences. Naturalist Rachel Carson described vividly one such consequence in her widely read book Silent Spring. *Abridged from Rachel Carson,* Silent Spring *(Boston, 1962), 103–4.*

OVER INCREASINGLY large areas of the United States, spring now comes unheralded by the return of the birds, and the early mornings are strangely silent where once they were filled with the beauty of bird song. This sudden silencing of the song of birds, this obliteration of the color and beauty and interest they lend to our world have come about swiftly, insidiously, and unnoticed by those whose communities are as yet unaffected.

From the town of Hinsdale, Illinois, a housewife wrote in despair to one of the world's leading ornithologists, Robert Cushman Murphy, Curator Emeritus of Birds at the American Museum of Natural History.

Marine biologist Rachel Carson, whose book Silent Spring *drew attention to environmental pollution. (Courtesy of Erich Hartmann/Magnum Photos, Inc.)*

Here in our village the elm trees have been sprayed for several years [she wrote in 1958]. When we moved here six years ago, there was a wealth of bird life; I put up a feeder and had a steady stream of cardinals, chickadees, downies and nuthatches all winter, and the cardinals and chickadees brought their young ones in the summer.

After several years of DDT spray, the town is almost devoid of robins and starlings; chickadees have not been on my shelf for two years, and this year the cardinals are gone too; the nesting population in the neighborhood seems to consist of one dove pair and perhaps one catbird family.

It is hard to explain to the children that the birds have been killed off, when they have learned in school that a Federal law protects the birds from killing or capture. "Will they ever come back?" they ask, and I do not have the answer. The elms are still dying, and so are the birds. *Is* anything being done? *Can* anything be done? Can *I* do anything?

A year after the federal government had launched a massive spraying program against the fire ant, an Alabama woman wrote: "Our place has been a veritable bird sanctuary for over half a century. Last July we all remarked, 'There are more birds than ever.' Then, suddenly, in the second week of August, they all disappeared. I was accustomed to rising early to care for my favorite mare that had a young filly. There was not a sound of the song of a bird. It was eerie, terrifying. What was man doing to our perfect and beautiful world? Finally, five months later a blue jay appeared and a wren."

The autumn months to which she referred brought other somber reports from the deep South, where in Mississippi, Louisiana, and Alabama the *Field Notes* published quarterly by the National Audubon Society and the United States Fish and Wildlife Service noted the striking phenomenon of "blank spots weirdly empty of virtually *all* bird life." The *Field Notes* are a compilation of the reports of seasoned observers who have spent many years afield in their particular areas and have unparalleled knowledge of the normal bird life of the region. One such observer reported that in driving about southern Mississippi that fall she saw "no land birds at all for long distances." Another in Baton Rouge reported that the contents of her feeders had lain untouched "for weeks on end," while fruiting shrubs in her yard, that ordinarily would be stripped clean by that time, still were laden with berries. Still another reported that his picture window, "which often used to frame a scene splashed with the red of 40 or 50 cardinals and crowded with other species, seldom permitted a view of as many as a bird or two at a time." Professor Maurice Brooks of the University of West Virginia, an authority on the birds of the Appalachian region, reported that the West Virginia bird population had undergone "an incredible reduction."

Questions

1. *Which aspects of the 1950s seem most familiar today? The least familiar?*
2. *Who in American society appears to have gained the most from the fifties system? Who the least? What explains those results?*
3. *The fifties has often been described as a "conservative" period in American history. Do you agree? Why or why not?*

FURTHER READING

For some differing perspectives on American life during the 1950s, see Eric F. Goldman, The Crucial Decade—And After: America, 1945–1960 *(New York, 1960); William E. Leuchtenburg,* A Troubled Feast: American Society Since 1945, *rev. ed. (Boston, 1979); Elaine Tyler May,* Homeward Bound: American Families in the Cold War Era *(New York, 1988); and Stephen J. Whitfield,* The Culture of the Cold War *(Baltimore, 1991).*

Nonviolence and the Civil Rights Movement

Penny A. Russell

INTRODUCTION

Some histories of the civil rights movement begin in 1954 with the Brown v. Board of Education *decision that struck down separate but equal in public education. Other writers insist that the movement began in August 1955 with the decision of an all-white Mississippi jury to set free the two white men who brutally tortured and murdered fourteen-year-old Chicago native Emmett Till for allegedly whistling at a white woman. Many scholars begin their analysis with Rosa Parks, Martin Luther King, Jr., and the Montgomery Bus Boycott that started in December 1955. Recently, a few scholars have searched for the origins of the movement in the decades before the 1950s.*

Historians also disagree on how to characterize the ideology, politics, strategies, and tactics of the movement. A few have insisted that the commonly used term "the civil rights movement" is inadequate because this social movement was concerned with more than securing citizenship rights for Blacks. Some people saw the movement as a search for community, others spoke of it as a religious crusade, and still others believed it was a battle for the soul of America. To understand how and why African-American activism and politics came to be one of the dominant forces in American life from the mid-1950s to the mid-1960s, you must understand the origins and the foundation of the civil rights movement.

African Americans attempted to mobilize mass movements before the 1950s. The first call for a march on Washington came in May 1941, twenty-two years before Martin Luther King, Jr., told the nation about his dream of equality for all people. In May 1941,

A. Philip Randolph urged African Americans to demonstrate in Washington for an end to discrimination in defense industries and in the military. The march was canceled only after President Franklin D. Roosevelt issued Executive Order 8802, which outlawed discrimination in employment in defense industries that held government contracts and created a Fair Employment Practices Committee (FEPC) to investigate companies that violated the order.

The mass movement that Randolph had wanted to create became a reality fourteen years later. On 1 December 1955, Rosa Parks left her seamstress job in a tailor shop, boarded a city bus for home, and was arrested for refusing to give up her seat to a white passenger, a violation of Alabama's segregation laws. In response, the Women's Political Council, a black women's organization that had been petitioning Montgomery's mayor about discrimination and segregation on the city buses, called for a boycott of the buses on 5 December when Parks's case went to trial. E. D. Nixon and other black men in Montgomery met to discuss the situation and they endorsed the idea of a boycott and called for a mass meeting on the night of 5 December as well.

The city buses were virtually empty of black riders on the morning of the boycott. That same afternoon, Nixon and other male leaders created the Montgomery Improvement Association and elected a young minister, Martin Luther King, Jr., as head of the organization. African Americans in Montgomery walked for a year, enduring intimidation, loss of employment, violence, and bombings until the U.S. Supreme Court declared Montgomery's bus segregation laws unconstitutional.

African-American college students became the leaders and innovators during the next phase of the movement. On 1 February 1960, Franklin McCain, David Richmond, Joseph McNeil, and Izell Blair, Jr., four black college students attending North Carolina Agricultural and Technical College in Greensboro, asked to be served at a Woolworth's lunch counter and refused to leave their seats when they were denied service. Their actions sparked sit-ins by black college students, who were sometimes joined by a few white students, all across the South. In mid-April 1960 local student sit-in leaders met at Shaw University in Raleigh, North Carolina, and, with the assistance of Ella Baker of the Southern Christian Leadership Conference (SCLC), created the Student Nonviolent Coordinating Committee (SNCC) to organize their struggles against segregation.

SNCC's first efforts to register African-American voters were in McComb, Mississippi, under the direction of Robert Moses, a Harlem school teacher who had attended graduate school at Harvard and who had worked with Ella Baker in the past. Despite intimidation, humiliation, violence, and arrests, SNCC members worked with local activists to establish voting rights projects in other communities in Mississippi where they supported the efforts of African Americans to register to vote. SNCC workers were often arrested for their actions and chose to serve their sentences instead of accepting bail. This was a dangerous choice, for African Americans were routinely beaten and mistreated in southern jails.

In April 1963, Martin Luther King, Jr., was arrested in Birmingham, Alabama. While he was incarcerated, in response to a letter from white clergymen, he composed the most famous statement on the philosophy of nonviolent direct action. They had accused King and the SCLC of promoting violence and argued that civil rights activists were outsiders who should not have come to the city. In his letter from jail, King explained the use of nonviolence and assured the clergymen that they would join African Americans in their protests if they knew how the police had tortured Blacks both in the streets and the jails of Birmingham.

Most African-American organizations involved in the struggle for social and political change from the mid-1950s to the mid-1960s adopted the philosophy of nonviolence and the tactics of nonviolent direct action. The definition of nonviolence and how it should be used differed from individual to individual and from group to group, but most civil rights activists agreed on the goals of their movement. They wanted to destroy segregation and transform the nation. They embraced the spirit of urgency that Martin Luther King, Jr., spoke about at the August 1963 March on Washington: "Now is the time to make real the promises of democracy; now is the time to rise from the dark and desolate valley of *segregation to the sunlit path of racial justice; now is the time to lift our nation from the quicksands of racial justice to the solid rock of brotherhood; now is the time to make justice a reality for all God's children."*

THE STRATEGIES OF NONVIOLENCE
AND THE DANGERS OF ACTIVISM

These documents offer different views of nonviolence, activism, and resistance by African Americans. Some of these people, such as Rosa Parks, Malcolm X, and King, are familiar while others, such as Ella Baker, James Forman, or A. Philip Randolph, are not. These selections are a small example of the creativity and innovation that activists employed in their efforts to transform the United States into a nation where all citizens could enjoy justice, equality, and freedom.

A. Philip Randolph Calls for a March on Washington, 1941

A. Philip Randolph was the head of the Brotherhood of Sleeping Car Porters, a predominantly African-American labor union, an early civil rights activist, and publisher of The Black Worker, *a labor magazine. In this excerpt from his May 1941 call for a march on Washington, Randolph wanted "mass action that is orderly and lawful, but aggressive and militant, for justice, equality and freedom."*

Taken from "To March On Washington for Jobs and Equal Participation in National Defense," The Black Worker, *May 1941, p. 4.*

Greetings:

We call upon you to fight for jobs in National Defense.

We call upon you to struggle for the integration of Negroes in the armed forces, such as the Air Corps, Navy, Army and Marine Corps of the Nation.

We call upon you to demonstrate for the abolition of Jim-Crowism in all Government departments and defense employment.

This is an hour of crisis. It is a crisis of democracy. It is a crisis of minority groups. It is a crisis of Negro Americans.

What is this crisis?

To American Negroes, it is the denial of jobs in Government defense projects. It is racial discrimination in Government departments. It is widespread Jim-Crowism in the armed forces of the nation. . . .

What shall we do? . . .

With faith and confidence of the Negro people in their own power for self-liberation, Negroes can break down the barriers of discrimination against employment in National Defense. . . .

Most important and vital to all, Negroes, by the mobilization and coordination of their mass power, can cause PRESIDENT ROOSEVELT TO ISSUE AN EXECUTIVE ORDER ABOLISHING DISCRIMINATIONS IN ALL GOVERNMENT DEPARTMENTS, ARMY, NAVY, AIR CORPS AND NATIONAL DEFENSE JOBS. . . .

In this period of power politics, nothing counts but pressure, more pressure, and still more pressure, through the tactic and strategy of broad, organized, aggressive mass action behind the vital and important issues of the Negro. To this end, we propose that ten thousand Negroes MARCH ON WASHINGTON FOR JOBS IN NATIONAL DEFENSE AND EQUAL INTEGRATION IN THE FIGHTING FORCES OF THE UNITED STATES.

An "all-out" thundering march on Washington, ending in a monster and huge demonstration at Lincoln's Monument will shake up white America.

It will shake up official Washington.

It will give encouragement to our white friends to fight all the harder by our side, with us, for our righteous cause.

It will gain respect for the Negro people.

It will create a new sense of self-respect among Negroes. . . .

We summon you to mass action that is orderly and lawful, but aggressive and militant, for justice, equality and freedom.

From "To March on Washington for Jobs and Equal Participation in National Defense" by A. Philip Randolph as it appeared in *The Black Worker*, p. 4, May 1941.

Rosa L. Parks is Arrested in Montgomery, Alabama on 1 December 1955

In a 1977 interview Rosa Parks remembers that she told the city bus driver to "go on and have me arrested" for not giving up her seat to a white man who boarded the bus after her. In this selection, she discusses the events that ignited a community-wide protest.

Taken from Howell Raines, My Soul Is Rested: Movement Days in the Deep South Remembered *(New York, 1977), 40-42.*

As I got up on the bus and walked to the seat I saw there was only one vacancy that was just back of where it was considered the white section. So this was the seat I that I took, next to the aisle, and a man was sitting next to me. . . . The third stop is when all the front seats were taken, and this one man was standing and when the driver looked around and saw he was standing, he asked the four of us, the man in the seat with me and the two women across the aisle, to let him have those front seats.

At his first request, didn't any of us move. Then he spoke again and said, "You'd better make it light on yourselves and let me have those seats." At this point, of course, the passenger who would have taken the seat hadn't said anything. In fact, he never did speak to my knowledge. When the three people, the man who was in the seat with me and the two women, stood up and moved into the aisle, I remained where I was. When the driver saw that I was still sitting there, he asked if I was going to stand up. I told him no, I wasn't. He said, "Well, if you don't stand up, I'm going to have you arrested." I told him to go on and have me arrested.

He got off the bus and came back shortly. A few minutes later, two policemen got on the bus, and they approached me and asked if the driver had asked me to stand up, and I said yes, and they wanted to know why I didn't. I told them I didn't think I should have to stand up. After I had paid my fare and occupied a seat, I didn't think I should have to give it up. They placed me under arrest then and had me to get in the police car, and I was taken to jail and booked on suspicion, I believe. The questions were asked, the usual questions they ask a prisoner or somebody that's under arrest. They had to determine whether or not the driver wanted to press charges or swear out a warrant, which he did. Then they took me to jail and I was placed in a cell. In a little while I was taken from the cell, and my picture was made and fingerprints taken. I went back to the cell then, and a few minutes later I was called back again, and when this happened I found out that Mr. E.D. Nixon and Attorney and Mrs. Clifford Durr had come to make bond for me.

In the meantime before this, of course . . . I was given permission to make a telephone call after my picture was taken and fingerprints taken. I called my home and spoke to my mother on the telephone and told her what had happened, that I was in jail. She was quite upset and asked me had the police beaten me. I told her, no, I hadn't been physically injured, but I was being held in jail, and I wanted my husband to come and get me out. . . . He didn't have a car at that time, so he had to get someone to bring him down. At the time when he got down, Mr. Nixon and the Durrs had just made bond for me, so we all met at the jail and we went home.

Student Nonviolent Coordinating Committee Statement of Purpose

The Reverend James Lawson was a divinity student who was expelled from Vanderbilt University after sit-ins in the spring of 1960. Later that year he would be influential in the founding of the Student Nonviolent Coordinating Committee. In May 1960, he drafted the statement of purpose for the new organization that appeared in the first issue of the newspaper the students created, The Student Voice 1 *(June 1960): 1.*

Statement of Purpose

"Carrying out the mandate of the Raleigh Conference to write a statement of purpose for the movement, the Temporary Student Nonviolent Coordinating Committee submits for careful consideration the following draft. We urge all local state or regional groups to examine it closely. Each member of our movement must work diligently to understand the depths of <u>nonviolence</u>.

We affirm the philosophical or religious ideal of nonviolence as the foundation of our purpose, the pre-supposition of our faith, and the manner of our action. Nonviolence as it grows from Judaic-Christian tradition seeks a social order of justice permeated by love. Integration of human endeavor represents the crucial first step towards such a society.

Through nonviolence, courage displaces fear; love transforms hate. Acceptance dissipates prejudice; hope ends despair. Peace dominates war; faith reconciles doubt. Mutual regards cancel enmity. Justice for all overthrows injustice. The redemptive community supercedes [supersedes] systems of gross social immorality.

Love is the central motif of nonviolence. Love is the force by which God binds man to himself and man to man. Such love goes to the extreme; it remains loving and forgiving even in the midst of hostility. It matches the capacity of evil to inflict suffering with an even more enduring capacity to absorb evil, all the while persisting in love.

By appealing to conscience and standing on the moral nature of human existence, nonviolence nurtures the atmosphere in which reconciliation and justice become actual possibilities."

Prepared by-Rev. J.M. Lawson, Jr. Saturday, May 14, 1960

Bigger Than A Hamburger

Ella Baker, executive director of the Southern Christian Leadership Conference, organized the student conference in Raleigh, North Carolina, from which SNCC emerged. She encouraged the student leaders attending the Raleigh conference to create their own organization where they would be free to work "to rid America of the scourge of racial segregation and discrimination—not only at lunch counters, but in every aspect of life."

From "Statement of Purpose" by Rev. James Lawson as it appeared in *The Student Voice*, June 1960.

Baker's ideas about leadership and community organizing were adopted by SNCC and they are presented in Ella J. Baker, "Bigger Than A Hamburger," Southern Patriot (June 1960): 1.

Raleigh, N.C.—The Student Leadership Conference made it crystal clear that current sit-ins and other demonstrations are concerned with something bigger than a hamburger or even a giant-sized Coke.

Whatever may be the difference in approach to their goal, the Negro and white students, North and South, are seeking to rid America of the scourge of racial segregation and discrimination—not only at lunch counters, but in every aspect of life.

In reports, casual conversations, discussion groups, and speeches, the sense and spirit of the following statement that appeared in the initial newsletter of the students at Barer-Scotia College, concord, N.C., were re-echoed time and again:

We want the world to know that we no longer accept the inferior position of second-class citizenship. We are willing to go to jail, be ridiculed, spat upon and even suffer physical violence to obtain First Class Citizenship.

By and large, this feeling that they have a destined date with freedom, was not limited to a drive for personal freedom for the Negro in the South. Repeatedly it was emphasized that the movement was concerned with the moral implications of racial discrimination for the "whole world" and the "Human Race."

"This universality of approach was linked with a perceptive recognition that "it is important to keep the movement democratic and to avoid struggles for personal leadership."

It was further evident that desire for supportive cooperation from adult leaders and the adult community was also tempered by apprehension that adults might try to "capture" the student movement. The students showed willingness to be met on the basis of equality, but were intolerant of anything that smacked of manipulation or domination.

This inclination toward group-centered leadership, rather than toward a leader-centered group pattern of organization, was refreshing indeed to those of the older group who bear the scars of

---

From "Bigger Than A Hamburger" by Ella J. Baker as it appeared in *The Southern Patriot*, June 1960.

the battle, the frustrations and the disillusionment that come when the prophetic leader turns out to have heavy feet of clay.

However hopeful might be the signs in the direction of group-centeredness, the fact that many schools and communities, especially in the South, have not provided adequate experience for young Negroes to assume the initiative and think and act independently accentuated the need for guarding the student movement against well-meaning, but nevertheless unhealthy, overprotectiveness.

Here is an opportunity for adult and youth to work together and provide genuine leadership—the development of the individual to his highest potential for the benefit of the group. . . .

In Jail in Greenwood, Mississippi

James Forman provides the following glimpse of life for SNCC activists in the Greenwood, Mississippi jail in his book The Making of Black Revolutionaries: A Personal Account *(New York, 1972), 299-301.*

April 2, 1963: We have been in jail one week today. Our morale is good, although there are serious undertones of a desire to be free among some members of the group. . . .

The cell in which we are being held is not so bad so far as American prisons go. (The entire penal system needs reforming.) We are eight in a cell with six bunks. We have two mattresses on the floor. There is an open shower, a sink, a stool. It took us two days to get a broom and five days to get some salt for our food. The inner cell in which we are "contained" is approximately 15' x 12'. Not much room is there? . . .

We are also improving our minds. We have been allowed to keep our books and we have sufficient cigarettes. I even have my pipe and some tobacco. Personally, I have tried to organize our lives. Do you expect anything else of me? We have occasional classes. Moses gave us an excellent math lecture the other day. I gave one lesson in writing and English. Guyot has delivered several in biology. We are always having discussions. Sometimes one of us will read a passage from a book and then we will discuss the meaning of it. We have had several stimulating conversations on Thoreau's essay on Civil Disobedience and Nkrumah's thoughts on Positive Action. . . .

My personal opinion as to the significance of our staying in jail follows: I am convinced that all the people connected with SNCC are busily engaged in protesting our unjust imprisonment. This is as it should be. I am also convinced that others sympathetic to the cause of Freedom are also alarmed at this travesty of justice. Only our bodies are confined to this cell. Our minds are free to think what we wish and we know our stay here will also pass away. Our imprisonment serves to dramatize to the nation and to the world that the black man does not even have the right to *try* to be an American citizen in some parts of our so-called democracy. Our jail-without-bail may also serve to remind others in the movement of the need for some of us to stay in jail to dramatize the situation.

On a local and state level it is important that we stay in jail, for people are remembered more by what they do than by what they say. We have been telling Mississippians that we must prepare to die. We have encouraged them to accept our beliefs. Thus it follows that we must lead by example rather than by words.

Letter from the Birmingham City Jail

King presents his ideas on the use of nonviolence and reminds the white clergymen that he is in Birmingham because "injustice anywhere is a threat to justice everywhere." This version of his famous letter is in Martin Luther King, Jr., "Letter from Birmingham Jail," in Why We Can't Wait *(New York, 1963), 77-83, 98-100.*

April 16, 1963

MY DEAR FELLOW CLERGYMEN:
While confined here in the Birmingham city jail, I came across your recent statement calling my present activities "unwise and

untimely." Seldom do I pause to answer criticism of my work and ideas. If I sought to answer all the criticisms that cross my desk, my secretaries would have little time for anything other than such correspondence in the course of the day, and I would have no time for constructive work. But since I feel that you are men of genuine good will and that your criticisms are sincerely set forth, I want to try to answer your statement in what I hope will be patient and reasonable terms.

I think I should indicate why I am here in Birmingham, since you have been influenced by the view which argues against "outsiders coming in." . . . Several months ago the [local SCLC] affiliate here in Birmingham asked us to be on call to engage in a nonviolent direct-action program if such were deemed necessary. We readily consented, and when the hour came we lived up to our promise. So I, along with several members of my staff, am here because I was invited here. I am here because I have organizational ties here.

But more basically, I am in Birmingham because injustice is here. . . .

Moreover, I am cognizant of the interrelatedness of all communities and states. I cannot sit idly by in Atlanta and not be concerned about what happens in Birmingham. Injustice anywhere is a threat to justice everywhere. We are caught in an inescapable network of mutuality, tied in a single garment of destiny. Whatever affects one directly, affects all indirectly. Never again can we afford to live with the narrow, provincial "outside agitator" idea. Anyone who lives inside the United States can never be considered an outsider anywhere within its bounds.

You deplore the demonstrations taking place in Birmingham. But your statement, I am sorry to say, fails to express a similar concern for the conditions that brought about the demonstrations. . . .

In any nonviolent campaign there are four basic steps: collection of the facts to determine whether injustices exist; negotiation; self-purification; and direct action. We have gone through all these steps in Birmingham. There can be no gainsaying the fact that racial injustice engulfs this community. Birmingham is probably the most thoroughly segregated city in the United States. Its ugly record of brutality is widely known. Negroes have experienced grossly unjust treatment in the courts. There have been more unsolved bombings of Negro homes and churches in Birmingham than in any other city in the nation. These are the hard, brutal facts of the case. On the basis of these conditions, Negro leaders sought to negotiate with the city fathers. But the latter consistently refused to engage in good-faith negotiation. . . .

You may well ask: "Why direct action? Why sit-ins, marches and so forth? Isn't negotiation a better path?" You are quite right in calling for negotiation. Indeed, this is the very purpose of direct action. Nonviolent direct action seeks to create such a crisis and foster such a tension that a community which has constantly refused to negotiate is forced to confront the issue. It seeks so to dramatize the issue that it can no longer be ignored. . . .

. . . My friends, I must say to you that we have not made a single gain in civil rights without determined legal and nonviolent pressure. Lamentably, it is an historical fact that privileged groups seldom give up their privileges voluntarily. . . .

We know through painful experience that freedom is never voluntarily given by the oppressor; it must be demanded by the oppressed. Frankly, I have yet to engage in a direct-action campaign that was "well timed" in the view of those who have not suffered unduly from the disease of segregation. For years now I have heard the word "Wait!" It rings in the ear of every Negro with piercing familiarity. This "Wait" has almost always meant "Never." We must come to see, with one of our distinguished jurists, that "justice too long delayed is justice denied." . . .

Before closing, I feel impelled to mention one other point in your statement that has troubled me profoundly. You warmly commended the Birmingham police force for keeping "order" and "preventing violence." I doubt that you would have so warmly commended the police force if you had seen its dogs sinking their teeth into unarmed, nonviolent Negroes. I doubt that you would so quickly commend the policemen if you were to observe their ugly and inhumane treatment of Negroes here in the city jail; if you were to watch them push and curse old Negro women and young Negro girls; if you were to see them slap and kick old Negro men and young boys; if you were to observe them, as they did on two occasions, refuse to give us food because we wanted to sing our grace together. I cannot join you in your praise of the Birmingham police department. . . .

I wish you had commended the Negro sit-inners and demonstrators of Birmingham for their sublime courage, their willingness to suffer and their amazing discipline in the midst of great provocation. One day the South will recognize its real heroes. They will be the James Merediths, with the noble sense of purpose that enables them to face jeering and hostile mobs, and with the agonizing loneliness that characterizes the life of the pioneer. They will be old, oppressed, battered Negro women, symbolized in a seventy-two-year-old woman in Montgomery, Alabama, who rose up with a sense of dignity and with her people decided not to ride segregated buses, and who responded with ungrammatical profundity to one who inquired about her weariness: "My feets is tired, but my soul is at rest." They will be the young high school and college students, the young ministers of the gospel and a host of their elders, courageously and nonviolently sitting in at lunch counters and willingly going to jail for conscience' sake. One day the South will know that when these disinherited children of God sat down at lunch counters, they were in reality standing up for what is best in the American dream and for the most sacred values in our Judaeo-Christian heritage, thereby bringing our nation back to those great wells of democracy which were dug deep by the founding fathers in their formulation of the Constitution and the Declaration of Independence. . . .

. . . Let us all hope that the dark clouds of racial prejudice will soon pass away and the deep fog of misunderstanding will be lifted from our fear-drenched communities, and in some not too distant tomorrow the radiant stars of love and brotherhood will shine over our great nation with all their scintillating beauty.

Yours for the cause of Peace and Brotherhood,
MARTIN LUTHER KING, JR.

To Mississippi Youth from Malcolm X

Malcolm X, originally Malcolm Little, took the surname X to represent the lost identity of African slaves. Malcolm became the main spokesman for the Nation of Islam during the 1950s. While in the Nation of Islam, he emphasized racial separatism and black self-reliance and was described by some as militant and extremist. He became disillusioned with and left the Nation of Islam in March 1964 and subsequently founded the Organization of Afro-American Unity (OAAU). From his break with the Nation of Islam in 1964 until his assassination in February 1965, he distanced himself from racial separatism and sought solidarity with the civil rights movement. In this excerpt from a speech on 31 December 1964, Malcolm presents his views on nonviolence and the movement in Mississippi.

Excerpted from Malcolm X, "To Mississippi Youth," in George Breitman, ed., Malcolm X Speaks: Selected Speeches and Statements *(New York, 1965), 138, 142-44.*

My experience has been that in many instances where you find Negroes talking about nonviolence, they are not nonviolent with each other, and they're not loving with each other, or forgiving with each other. Usually when they say they're nonviolent, they mean they're nonviolent with somebody else. I think you understand what I mean. They are nonviolent with the enemy. A person can come to your home, and if he's white and wants to heap some kind of brutality on you, you're nonviolent. . . . But if another Negro just stomps his foot, you'll rumble with him in a minute. Which shows you that there's an inconsistency there.

I myself would go for nonviolence if it was consistent, if everybody was going to be nonviolent all the time. I'd say, okay, let's get with it, we'll all be nonviolent. But I don't go along with any kind of nonviolence unless everybody's going to be nonviolent. If they make the Ku Klux Klan nonviolent, I'll be nonviolent. If they make the White Citizens Council nonviolent, I'll be nonviolent. But as long as you've got somebody else not being nonviolent, I don't want anybody coming to me talking any nonviolent talk. . . .

In studying the process of this so-called [racial] progress during the past twenty years, we of the Organization of Afro-American Unity realized that the only time the black man in this country is given any kind of recognition, or even listened to, is when America is afraid of outside pressure, or when she's afraid of her image abroad. . . .

And today you'll find in the United Nations, and it's not an accident, that every time the Congo question or anything on the African continent is being debated, they couple it with what is going on, or what is happening to you and me, in Mississippi and Alabama and these other places. In my opinion, the greatest accomplishment that was made in the struggle of the black man in America in 1964 toward some kind of real progress was the successful linking together of our problem with the African problem, or making our problem a world problem. . . .

So we here in the Organization of Afro-American Unity are with the struggle in Mississippi one thousand per cent. We're with the efforts to register our people in Mississippi to vote one thousand per cent. But we do not go along with anybody telling us to help nonviolently. We think that if the government says that Negroes have a right to vote, and then some Negroes come out to vote, and some kind of Ku Klux Klan is going to put them in the river, and the government doesn't do anything about it, it's time for us to organize and band together and equip ourselves and qualify ourselves to protect ourselves. And once you can protect yourself, you don't have to worry about being hurt. . . .

If you don't have enough people down there to do it, we'll come down there and help you do it. Because we're tired of this old runaround that our people have been given in this country. For a long time they accused me of not getting involved in politics. They should've been glad I didn't get involved in politics, because anything I get in, I'm in it all the way. If they say we don't take part in the Mississippi struggle, we will organize brothers here in New York who know how to handle these kind of affairs, and they'll slip into Mississippi like Jesus slipped into Jerusalem.

Questions

1. *How did these people and organizations use nonviolent direct action? Do they have similar ideas about nonviolence?*
2. *What are some of the dangers that activists in the movement faced?*

3. *Did King and his allies, members of SNCC, and Malcolm X understand each others' views on nonviolence and activism? Was there any common ground between them?*
4. *Do these documents suggest that some people were more idealistic in the 1950s and 1960s? Why or why not?*
5. *Do you think that you could have been an activist like any of these people? What factors would encourage or inhibit you?*

FURTHER READING

Race & Democracy: The Civil Rights Struggle in Louisiana, 1915-1972 by Adam Fairclough (Athens, 1995) demonstrates that civil rights struggles began with the twentieth century. Two studies that analyze the indigenous roots of the movement and emphasize the roles of local leaders are Charles M. Payne, *I've Got the Light of Freedom: The Organizing Tradition and the Mississippi Freedom Struggle* (Berkeley, 1995); and John Dittmer, *Local People: The Struggle for Civil Rights in Mississippi* (Urbana, 1994). The best history of SNCC is still Clayborne Carson, *In Struggle: SNCC and the Black Awakening of the 1960s* (Cambridge, 1995); and there is a collection of fascinating interviews with organizers in *A Circle of Trust: Remembering SNCC*, ed. Cheryl Lynn Greenberg (New Brunswick, 1998). *But for Birmingham: The Local and National Movements in the Civil Rights Struggle* by Glenn T. Eskew (Chapel Hill, 1997) examines one of the most important civil rights campaigns of the 1960s. Belinda Robnett's *How Long? How Long? African-American Women in the Struggle for Civil Rights* (New York, 1997) is a long-awaited study of women's activism that provides a theoretical framework for exploring their unique roles in the movement. Biographies have provided some of the best scholarship on the movement, and the second volume of Taylor Branch's biography of King, *Pillar of Fire: America in the King Years, 1963-65* (New York, 1998), is now available. The life of a significant, but overlooked, woman who was responsible for running SNCC is eloquently presented in Cynthia Griggs Fleming, *Soon We Will Not Cry: The Liberation of Ruby Doris Smith Robinson* (Lanham, Maryland, 1998). A thoughtful comparison of the ideas of King and Malcolm X can be found in James H. Cone, *Martin & Malcolm & America: A Dream or a Nightmare* (Maryknoll, New York, 1992).

Dissent in the 1960s: Definitions and Context

Steven Conn

INTRODUCTION

Sex, drugs, and rock 'n roll.

For many people this has become the easiest way to summarize the tumultuous decade of the 1960s. Perhaps the most enduring images of those times remain hippies, flower children, rock music festivals, and be-ins. Needless to say this assessment of the decade as one dominated by dope-smoking hippies vastly oversimplifies. It obscures much about the nature of the dissent that took place during the 1960s. The easiest way to understand the nature of that dissent, and its role in shaping the 1960s, is to recognize and delineate three broad streams of youth and student activity that converged during the decade.

The first of these streams found its source in the American South and in the struggle for civil rights. Initially this movement based itself in black churches and other community institutions. Throughout the 1950s, the Southern Christian Leadership Conference (SCLC) had been the organizational heart of the civil rights movement. In 1960, however, black students founded the Student Non-Violent Coordinating Committee (SNCC), and these younger activists would eventually challenge their elders for leadership of the movement. A year later, black college students led dramatic sit-ins at the segregated Woolworth's lunch counter in Greensboro, North Carolina. The success of these sit-ins inspired dozens of other such actions and boldly announced the arrival of a new generation of civil rights activists.

By the second half of the decade, that younger generation had grown impatient with the slow progress of the civil rights movement and angry with the violent white backlash. A militant wing of the black youth movement split from the older generation, following the banner of "Black Power." Under that banner, younger black activists experimented with increasingly militant and separatist politics, embodied most famously in the Black Panther Party, and with a variety of cultural expressions exploring ideas of black pride.

The second stream originated in Port Huron, Michigan. There, roughly fifty college students from Ivy League and Big Ten universities gathered to form Students for a Democratic Society (SDS) in 1962. Their founding document, the Port Huron Statement, offered an impassioned critique of an American society grown comfortably complacent. For these students, the nation they now inherited gorged itself on consumerism, and while it starved spiritually, it remained politically indifferent despite the ever-present threat of nuclear annihilation, and it trumpeted pompous patriotism even while black Americans fought their second-class status. SDS called on students to lead a reinvigoration of American politics through the mechanism of "participatory democracy." Hundreds of SDS chapters organized on campuses from coast to coast and these formed the backbone of what became known as the "New Left."

The third stream formed in this context. The counter culture made its unofficial national debut in the summer of 1967 in San Francisco. In that summer, thousands of young people flocked to the Bay area to participate in the "Summer of Love." The summer began with the Monterey Pop Festival in June, which proved to be the first large-scale counter-cultural musical event. Throughout the late 1960s, large music festivals became unofficial conventions for counter-cultural rebels. The musical event that seemed to demonstrate most dramatically the promise of the counter culture took place near Woodstock, New York, in August 1969. For the most enthusiastic participants in the counter culture, Woodstock stood as a gentle alternative to the rest of American society. Some participants called themselves "Woodstock Nation."

The legacy of the counter culture is complicated and is still unfolding. For many involved, the counter culture really meant nothing more than sex, drugs, and rock. At the same time, such glib dismissals do not do justice to the sincerity and creativity with which some experimented with different ways of living and the depth to which they explored the connection between the personal and the political. The varieties of personal expression that college students today take for granted have their origins in the explorations of the counter culture. The counter culture did, for better or worse, alter the American social landscape.

To separate dissent in the 1960s into these three categories reflects, at some level, a convenience for historians. Surely these three broad groups involved different people, dealt with different issues, and employed different methods to achieve their goals. But it is also important to recognize that they overlapped in significant ways as well. There were certainly black hippies and those who believed in communal living and political engagement. The job for the historian is to analyze both the differences and the similarities.

Voices From The 1960s

The young people who joined the various dissent movements of the 1960s made self-conscious efforts to define who they were and what they saw wrong with American society. Through poems, manifestos, books, and interviews they worked to explain their beliefs and to critique the social and political status quo. In the following selections, the leaders of the three main streams of dissent describe their goals and methods.

The Black Panther movement defined itself against the nonviolent tradition of the earlier civil rights movement. Stokely Carmichael and others rejected the methods of peaceful collaboration with white allies in favor of radical action. They linked racism, poverty, and America's foreign policy in Vietnam with the domestic repression of African Americans and called for armed struggle to replace the exploitative system.

Tom Hayden and other "New Left" activists believed in the possibility of constructive engagement in the political system as a means to create a more just society. Disillusioned with the perceived gap between American ideals and reality, these activists advocated wider political participation by the young in order to achieve social justice. Concentrating on the university as the focal point of activism, they hoped to bring these young people to the forefront of political mobilization.

Others rejected the possibility of constructive change in the status quo that the first two groups implicitly believed. Adherents of the "counter culture" movement called for either a complete disruption of "an insane society" or the rejection of society and a retreat to a separate and simple lifestyle.

FIRST STREAM:
SNCC, BLACK PANTHERS, BLACK CULTURE

"Black Power!"

During a march from Tennessee to Mississippi led by Martin Luther King, Jr., a small knot of young marchers refused to sing the civil rights movement's anthem "We Shall Overcome." Frustrated by the slow pace of civil rights progress, they decided to introduce a new slogan to the vocabulary of protest: "Black Power!" The young black activist Stokely Carmichael led this symbolic break with the older civil rights movement.

A member of the Student Non-Violent Coordinating Committee (SNCC) and eventually its head, Carmichael had soured on the possibilities of Gandhian non-violence to achieve racial equality and on the utility of working with white allies. In the selection below, Carmichael explains the philosophy of black power and its origins. Excerpted from Stokely Carmichael, "What We Want," New York Review of Books 7 (September 22, 1966): 5-7.

One of the tragedies of the struggle against racism is that up to now there has been no national organization which could speak to the growing militancy of young black people in the urban ghetto. There has been only a civil rights movement, whose tone of voice was adapted to an audience of liberal whites. It served as a sort of buffer zone between them and angry young blacks. None of its so-called leaders could go into a rioting community and be listened to. In a sense, I blame ourselves—together with the mass media—for what has happened in Watts, Harlem, Chicago, Cleveland, Omaha. Each time the people in those cities saw Martin Luther King get slapped, they became angry; when they saw four little black girls bombed to death, they were angrier; and when nothing

---

happened, they were steaming. We had nothing to offer that they could see, except to go out and be beaten again. We helped to build their frustration.

For too many years, black Americans marched and had their heads broken and got shot. . . . After years of this, we are at almost the same point—because we demonstrated from a position of weakness. We cannot be expected any longer to march and have our heads broken in order to say to whites: come on, you're nice guys. For you are not nice guys. We have found you out. . . .

An organization which claims to be working for the needs of a community—as SNCC does—must work to provide that community with a position of strength

Capturing a central paradox for African Americans in the 1960s, this demonstrator wonders why blacks should fight for a country which continued to deny them basic civil and political rights. In this way, the civil rights movement and the anti-war movement became two sides of the same coin. (Courtesy of Media Image Resource Alliance.)

from which to make its voice heard. This is the significance of black power beyond the slogan.

Black power can be clearly defined for those who do not attach the fears of white America to their questions about it. We should begin with the basic fact that black Americans have two problems: they are poor and they are black. All other problems arise from this two-sided reality: lack of education, the so-called apathy of black men. Any program to end racism must address itself to that double reality.

. . . Thus we determined to win political power, with the idea of moving on from there into activity that would have economic effects. With power, the masses could *make or participate in making* the decisions which govern their destinies, and thus create basic change in their day-to-day lives. . . .

. . . We have no infallible master plan and we make no claim to exclusive knowledge of how to end racism; different groups will work in their own different ways. SNCC cannot spell out the full logistics of self-determination but it can address itself to the problem by helping black communities define their needs, realize their strength, and go into action along a variety of lines which they must choose for themselves. Without knowing all the answers, it can address itself to the basic problem of poverty; to the fact that in . . . [one southern county] 86 white families own 90 per cent of the land. What are black people in that county going to do for jobs, where are they going to get money? There must be reallocation of land, of money.

Ultimately, the economic foundations of this country must be shaken if black people are to control their lives. The colonies of the United States—and this includes the black ghettoes within its borders, north and south—must be liberated. . . . For racism to die, a totally different America must be born.

This is what the white society does not wish to face; this is why that society prefers to talk about integration. But integration speaks not at all to the problem of poverty, only to the problem of blackness. Integration today means the man who "makes it," leaving his black brothers behind in the ghetto as fast as his new sports car will take him. It has no relevance to the Harlem wino or to the cotton-picker making three dollars a day. . . .

Integration, moreover, speaks to the problem of blackness in a despicable way. As a goal, it has been based on complete acceptance of the fact that *in order to have* a decent house or education, blacks must move into a white neighborhood or send their children to a white school. This reinforces, among both black and white, the idea that "white" is automatically better and "black" is by definition inferior. This is why integration is a subterfuge for the maintenance of white supremacy. It allows the nation to focus on a handful of Southern children who get into white schools, at great price, and to ignore the 94 per cent who are left behind in unimproved all-black schools. Such situations will not change until black people have power—to control their own school boards, in this case. Then Negroes become equal in a way that means something, and integration ceases to be a one-way street.

Then integration doesn't mean draining skills and energies from the ghetto into white neighborhoods; then it can mean white people moving from Beverly Hills into Watts. . . .

Whites will not see that I, for example, as a person oppressed because of my blackness, have common cause with other blacks who are oppressed because of blackness. . . .

The need for psychological equality is the reason why SNCC today believes that blacks must organize in the black community. Only black people can convey the revolutionary idea that black people are able to do things themselves. Only they can help create in the community an aroused and continuing black consciousness that will provide the basis for political strength. In the past, white allies have furthered white supremacy without the whites involved realizing it—or wanting it, I think. Black people must do things for themselves; they must get poverty money they will control and spend themselves, they must conduct tutorial programs themselves so that black children can identify with black people. This is one reason Africa has such importance: The reality of black men ruling their own natives gives blacks elsewhere a sense of possibility, of power, which they do not now have. . . .

Black people do not want to "take over" this country. They don't want to "get whitey"; they just want to get him off their backs, as the saying goes. . . .

But our vision is not merely of a society in which all black men have enough to buy the good things of life. When we urge that black money go into black pockets, we mean the communal pocket. We want to see money go back into the community and used to benefit it. . . . The society we seek to build among black people, then, is not a capitalist one. It is a society in which the spirit of community and humanistic love prevail. . . . We can build a community of love only where we have the ability and power to do so: among blacks.

As for white America, perhaps it can stop crying out against "black supremacy," "black nationalism," "racism in reverse," and begin facing reality. The reality is that this nation, from top to bottom, is racist; that racism is not primarily a problem of "human relations" but of an exploitation maintained—either actively or through silence—by the society as a whole.

The Black Panther Party

One of the most spectacular and controversial outgrowths of the Black Power movement was the Black Panther Party. Founded in 1966 by Huey Newton and Bobby Seale in Oakland, the party attracted a great deal of media attention for its commitment to armed self-defense. The image of the Panther dressed in military fatigues and armed became for many white Americans their worst nightmare of Black Power.

The party did not only attract media attention. The Panthers were hounded by the police and the FBI almost everywhere they established chapters. These encounters often led to violent, tragic encounters, many provoked by the police. Panthers were routinely harassed, arrested, and on several occasions, killed.

The media focus on the party's militancy also obscured the positive work many members did in inner-city communities, especially in Chicago where the party ran a successful school breakfast program for needy children.

In this excerpt from a 1973 interview, founder Huey Newton describes the Panther ethos of using armed violence to achieve political goals. His discussion of the "doomed" revolutionary   now seems poignantly ironic—Newton died in a drug-related shoot-out in 1989. Taken from "Playboy Interview: Huey Newton," 20 Playboy *(May 1973): 76, 78, 90.*

PLAYBOY: Do you think the *only* way to achieve your revolutionary goals is through armed violence?

NEWTON: Yes, and I think that ultimately it will be through armed violence, because the American ruling circle will not give up without a bitter struggle. But America will not be changed until the world is changed. To say that change will come here just through the ballot box would be a fantasy. We're running for city-council offices today. But if you ask if we would be prepared to fight with armed force when the time is right, I would say yes, when the occasion presents itself—and I think it will come, at some point in the future. . . .

From "Playboy Interview: Huey Newton" *Playboy*, Vol. 20 (May 1973). Reprinted by permissionof *Playboy*.

PLAYBOY: So you would feel no hesitation about using violence as a tool, even to the point of killing people, provided it advanced your movement or your principles?

NEWTON: That's right.

PLAYBOY: And you say that without reservation?

NEWTON: The death of any man diminishes me, but sometimes we may have to be diminished before we can reconstruct.

PLAYBOY: That raises our last question: If you're ready to kill for the cause, you must also be ready to die for it. Are you?

NEWTON: I will fight until I die, however that may come. But whether I'm around or not to see it happen, I know we will eventually succeed, not just in America but all over the world, in our struggle for the liberation of all oppressed peoples. The revolution will win. But [Russian revolutionary anarchist Mikhail] Bakunin wrote that the first lesson the revolutionary *himself* must learn is that he's a doomed man. If that sounds defeatist, you don't understand the nature of revolution: that it's an ongoing process and that we don't get out of life alive, anyway. All we can do as individuals is try to make things better now, for eventually we all die. I think Mao's statement sums it up best: "Death comes to everyone, but it varies in its significance. To die for the reactionary is as light as a feather. But to die for the revolution is heavier than Mount Tai."

The Black Panthers achieved the highest profile of any of the militant black power organizations. As a consequence, they often found themselves in conflict with the police. Here volunteers raise money to support Panther members about to go on trial. (Courtesy of Leonard Freed/Magnum Photos, Inc.)

Black Power and Black Culture

Black Power and black pride served as the wellspring for extraordinary cultural, as well as political, achievements. A new-found desire to celebrate black heritage, black history, and black culture helped heal some of the psychological damage inflicted on American blacks by generations of denying or denigrating their traditions. No one articulated this sensibility better than James Brown when he sang: "Say it strong, say it loud / I'm black and I'm proud."

Nikki Giovanni is one of a host of black writers who found their voice in the Black Power struggles of the 1960s. In this poem, written in 1968, she describes how the accumulated effects of violence against leaders for peace and justice transformed her personally. Taken from Nikki Giovanni, Black Feeling, Black Talk, Black Judgement *(New York, 1979), 68-70.*

Adulthood
(For Claudia)

i usta wonder who i'd be
when i was a little girl in indianapolis
sitting on doctors porches with post-dawn pre-debs
(wondering would my aunt drag me to church sunday)
i was meaningless
and i wondered if life
would give me a chance to mean

i found a new life in the withdrawal from all things
not like my image

when i was a teen-ager i usta sit
on front steps conversing
the gym teacher's son with embryonic eyes

Text, "Adulthood (For Claudia)", from *Black Feeling, Black Talk, Black Judgement* by Nikki Giovanni. Copyright © 1968, 1970 by Nikki Giovanni. Reprinted by permission of William Morrow & Co., Inc.

about the essential essence of the universe
(and other bullshit stuff)
recognizing the basic powerlessness of me

but then i went to college where i learned
that just because everything i was was unreal
i could be real and not just real through withdrawal
into emotional crosshairs or colored bourgeois
intellectual pretensions
but from involvement with things approaching reality
i could possibly have a life

so catatonic emotions and time wasting sex games
were replaced with functioning commitments to logic
and
necessity and the gray area was slowly darkened into
a Black thing

for a while progress was being made along with a certain
degree
of happiness cause i wrote a book and found a love
and organized a theatre and even gave some lectures on
Black history
and began to believe all good people could get
together and win without bloodshed
then
hammarskjöld was killed
and lumumba was killed
and diem was killed
and kennedy was killed
and malcolm was killed
and evers was killed
and schwerner, chaney and goodman were killed
and liuzzo was killed
and stokely fled the country
and le roi was arrested
and rap was arrested
and pollard, thompson and cooper were killed
and king was killed
and kennedy was killed
and i sometimes wonder why i didn't become a

debutante
sitting on porches, going to church all the time,
wondering
is my eye make-up on straight
or a withdrawn discoursing on the stars and moon
instead of a for real Black person who must now feel
and inflict
pain

[Note: Dag Hammarskjöld, United Nations Secretary General, 1961; Patrice Lumumba, Prime Minister of Congo, 1961; Ngo Dinh Diem, President of South Vietnam, 1963; President John F. Kennedy, 1963; Malcolm X, black nationalist leader, 1965; Medgar Evers, NAACP official, 1963; Michael Schwerner, James Chaney, Andrew Goodman, volunteers in Mississippi "Freedom Summer," a black voter registration project, 1964; Viola Liuzzo, white civil rights worker in Alabama, 1965; Stokely Carmichael, SNCC; Leroi Jones, black activist and playwright; H. Rap Brown, SNCC; Martin Luther King, Jr., civil rights leader, 1968; Robert F. Kennedy, Democratic presidential candidate, 1968.]

SECOND STREAM: STUDENTS AND THE "NEW LEFT"

The Port Huron Statement

The Port Huron Statement was the result of a conference held in Port Huron, Michigan, in 1962. Written largely by Tom Hayden, the statement offers a critique of American society and a call to action for America's students. The statement became the founding document for the Students for a Democratic Society, and it announced the arrival of the "New Left" in this country. Excerpted from "An Official Statement of Students for a Democratic Society," in How Democratic Is America? Responses to the New Left Challenge, *ed. Robert A. Goldwin (Chicago, 1969), 1-3, 5-15.*

INTRODUCTION: AGENDA FOR A GENERATION

We are people of this generation, bred in at least modest comfort, housed now in universities, looking uncomfortably to the world we inherit.

When we were kids, the United States was the wealthiest and strongest country in the world: the only one with the atom bomb, the least scarred by modern war, an initiator of the United Nations that we thought would distribute Western influence throughout the world. Freedom and equality for each individual, government of, by, and for the people—these American values we found good, principles by which we could live as men. Many of us began maturing in complacency.

As we grew, however, our comfort was penetrated by events too troubling to dismiss. First, the permeating and victimizing fact of human degradation, symbolized by the Southern struggle against racial bigotry, compelled most of us from silence to activism. Second, the enclosing fact of the Cold War, symbolized by the presence of the Bomb, brought awareness that we ourselves, and our friends, and millions of abstract "others" we knew more directly because of our common peril, might die at any time. We might deliberately ignore, or avoid, or fail to feel all other human problems, but not these two, for these were too immediate and crushing in their impact, too challenging in the demand that we as individuals take the responsibility for encounter and resolution.

While these and other problems either directly oppressed us or rankled our consciences and became our own subjective concerns, we began to see complicated and disturbing paradoxes in our surrounding America. The declaration "all men are created equal . . ." rang hollow before the facts of Negro life in the South and the big cities of the North. The proclaimed peaceful intentions of the United States contradicted its economic and military investments in the Cold War status quo.

We witnessed, and continue to witness, other paradoxes. With nuclear energy whole cities can easily be powered, yet the dominant nation-states seem more likely to unleash destruction greater than that incurred in all wars of human history. Although our own technology is destroying old and creating new forms of social organization, men still tolerate meaningless work and idleness. While two-thirds of mankind suffers undernourishment, our own upper classes revel amidst superfluous abundance. Although world population is expected to double in forty years, the nations still tolerate anarchy as a major principle of international conduct and uncontrolled exploitation governs the sapping of the earth's physical resources. Although mankind desperately needs revolutionary leadership, America rests in national stalemate, its goals ambiguous and tradition-bound instead of informed and clear, its democratic system apathetic and manipulated rather than "of, by, and for the people." . . .

Some would have us believe that Americans feel contentment amidst prosperity—but might it not better be called a glaze above deeply felt anxieties about their role in the new world? And if these anxieties produce a developed indifference to human affairs, do they not as well produce a yearning to believe there *is* an alternative to the present, that something *can* be done to change circumstances in the school, the workplaces, the bureaucracies, the government? It is to this latter yearning, at once the spark and engine of change, that we direct our present appeal. The search for truly democratic alternatives to the present, and a commitment to social experimentation with them, is a worthy and fulfilling human enterprise, one which moves us and, we hope, others today. . . .

We regard *men* as infinitely precious and possessed of unfulfilled capacities for reason, freedom, and love. In affirming these principles we are aware of countering perhaps the dominant conceptions of man in the twentieth century: that he is a thing to be manipulated, and that he is inherently incapable of directing his own affairs. We oppose the depersonalization that reduces human beings to the status of things—if anything, the brutalities of the twentieth century teach that means and ends are intimately related, that vague appeals to "posterity" cannot justify the mutilations of the present. We oppose, too, the doctrine of human incompetence because it rests essentially on the modern fact that men have been "competently" manipulated into incompetence— we see little reason why men cannot meet with increasing skill the complexities and responsibilities of their situation, if society is organized not for minority, but for majority, participation in decision-making.

Men have unrealized potential for self-cultivation, self-direction, self-understanding, and creativity. It is this potential that we regard as crucial and to which we appeal, not to the human potentiality for violence, unreason, and submission to authority. The goal of man and society should be human independence: a concern not with the image of popularity but with finding a meaning in life that is personally authentic; a quality of mind not compulsively driven by a sense of powerlessness, nor one which unthinkingly adopts status values, nor one which represses all threats to its habits, but one which has full, spontaneous access to present and past experiences, one which easily unites the fragmented parts of personal history, one which openly faces problems which are troubling and unresolved; one with an intuitive awareness of possibilities, an active sense of curiosity, an ability and willingness to learn. . . .

We would replace power rooted in possession, privilege, or circumstance by power and uniqueness rooted in love, reflectiveness, reason, and creativity. As a *social system* we seek the establishment of a democracy of individual participation, governed by two central aims: that the individual share in those social decisions determining the quality and direction of his life; that society be organized to encourage independence in men and provide the media for their common participation.

In a participatory democracy, the political life would be based in several root principles:

that decision-making of basic social consequence be carried on by public groupings;

that politics be seen positively, as the art of collectively creating an acceptable pattern of social relations;

that politics has the function of bringing people out of isolation and into community, thus being a necessary, though not sufficient, means of finding meaning in personal life;

that the political order should serve to clarify problems in a way instrumental to their solution; it should provide outlets for the expression of personal grievance and aspiration; opposing views should be organized so as to illuminate choices and facilitate the attainment of goals; channels should be commonly available to relate men to knowledge and to power so that private problems—from bad recreation facilities to personal alienation—are formulated as general issues.

The economic sphere would have as its basis the principles:

that work should involve incentives worthier than money or survival. It should be educative, not stultifying; creative, not mechanical; self-directed, not manipulated, encouraging independence, a respect for others, a sense of dignity and a willingness to accept social responsibility, since it is this experience that has crucial influence on habits, perceptions, and individual ethics;

that the economic experience is so personally decisive that the individual must share in its full determination;

that the economy itself is of such social importance that its major resources and means of production should be open to democratic participation and subject to democratic social regulation. . . .

In social change or interchange, we find violence to be abhorrent because it requires generally the transformation of the target, be it a human being or a community of people, into a depersonalized object of hate. It is imperative that the means of violence be abolished and the institutions—local, national, international—that encourage nonviolence as a condition of conflict be developed. . . .

Almost no students value activity as citizens. Passive in public, they are hardly more idealistic in arranging their private lives. . . . "Students don't even give a damn about apathy," one has said. Apathy toward apathy begets a privately constructed universe, a place of systematic study schedules, two nights each week for beer, a girl or two, and early marriage; a framework infused with personality, warmth, and under control, no matter how unsatisfying otherwise. . . .

But apathy is not simply an attitude; it is a product of social institutions, and of the structure and organization of higher education itself. . . . Tragically, the university could serve as a significant source of social criticism and an initiator of new modes and molders of attitudes. But the actual intellectual effect of the college experience is hardly distinguishable from that of any other communications channel—say, a television set—passing on the stock truths of the day. Students leave college somewhat more "tolerant" than when they arrived, but basically unchallenged in their values and political orientations. With administrators ordering the institution, and faculty the curriculum, the student learns by his isolation to accept elite rule within the university, which prepares him to accept later forms of minority control. The real function of the educational system—as opposed to its more rhetorical function of "searching for truth"—is to impart the key information and styles that will help the student get by, modestly but comfortably, in the big society beyond. . . .

The very isolation of the individual—from power and community and ability to aspire—means the rise of a democracy without publics. With the great mass of people structurally remote and psychologically hesitant with respect to democratic institutions, those institutions themselves attenuate and become, in the fashion of the vicious circle, progressively less accessible to those few who aspire to serious participation in social affairs. The vital democratic connection between community and leadership, between the mass and the several elites, has been so wrenched and perverted that disastrous policies go unchallenged time and again. . . .

TOWARDS AMERICAN DEMOCRACY

Every effort to end the Cold War and expand the process of world industrialization is an effort hostile to people and institutions whose interests lie in perpetuation of the East-West military threat and the postponement of change in the "have not" nations of the world. Every such effort, too, is bound to establish greater democracy in America. The major goals of a domestic effort would be:

1. America must abolish its political party stalemate. . . .
2. Mechanisms of voluntary association must be created through which political information can be imparted and political participation encouraged. . . .
3. Institutions and practices which stifle dissent should be abolished, and the promotion of peaceful dissent should be actively promoted. . . .
4. Corporations must be made publicly responsible. . . .
5. The allocation of resources must be based on social needs. A truly "public sector" must be

established, and its nature debated and
planned. . . .
6. America should concentrate on its genuine social
priorities: abolish squalor, terminate neglect, and
establish an environment for people to live in with
dignity and creativeness. . . .

THE UNIVERSITY AND SOCIAL CHANGE

. . . The civil rights, peace, and student movements are too
poor and socially slighted, and the labor movement too quiescent,
to be counted with enthusiasm. From where else can power and
vision be summoned? We believe that the universities are an
overlooked seat of influence.

. . . Social relevance, the accessibility to knowledge, and internal openness—these together make the university a potential base
and agency in the movement of social change.

1. Any new left in America must be, in large measure, a left
    with real intellectual skills, committed to deliberativeness,
    honesty, and reflection as working tools. The university
    permits the political life to be an adjunct to the academic
    one, and action to be informed by reason.
2. A new left must be distributed in significant social roles
    throughout the country. The universities are distributed in
    such a manner.
3. A new left must consist of younger people who matured in
    the postwar world, and must be directed to the recruitment
    of younger people. The university is an obvious beginning
    point.
4. A new left must include liberals and socialists, the former
    for their relevance, the latter for their sense of thoroughgo-
    ing reforms in the system. The university is a more sensible
    place than a political party for these two traditions to begin
    to discuss their differences and look for political synthesis.
5. A new left must start controversy across the land, if na-
    tional policies and national apathy are to be reversed. The
    ideal university is a community of controversy, within
    itself and in its effects on communities beyond.
6. A new left must transform modern complexity into issues
    that can be understood and felt close-up by every human

being. It must give form to the feelings of helplessness and indifference, so that people may see the political, social, and economic sources of their private troubles and organize to change society. In a time of supposed prosperity, moral complacency, and political manipulation, a new left cannot rely on only aching stomachs to be the engine force of social reform. The case for change, for alternatives that will involve uncomfortable personal efforts, must be argued as never before. The university is a relevant place for all of these activities. . . .

The bridge to political power, though, will be built through genuine cooperation, locally, nationally, and internationally, between a new left of young people, and an awakening community of allies. In each community we must look within the university and act with confidence that we can be powerful, but we must look outwards to the less exotic but more lasting struggles for justice.

THIRD STREAM:
YIPPIES!, COMMUNES, COUNTER CULTURE

The Yippies! in Chicago, 1968

The demonstrations in Chicago during the 1968 Democratic Convention were initially conceived by the Yippies! who sought to turn politics into a theater of the absurd and in doing so attract media attention. Abbie Hoffman, Jerry Rubin, and Paul Krassner founded the Yippies!, and Krassner is credited with coining the name. In his essay "The Birth of the Yippie! Conspiracy," Krassner succinctly described the purpose of the Yippies!: "No more marches. No more rallies. No more speeches. The dialogue is over baby. . . . The goal now is to disrupt an insane society."

197

In the following selection, Abbie Hoffman describes the goals of the Yippies! and the plans for the demonstrations in Chicago. Taken from Abbie Hoffman, Revolution for the Hell of It *(New York, 1968), 102-3, 106-8.*

Last December [1967] a group of us in New York conceived the Yippie! idea. We had four main objectives:

1. The blending of pot and politics into a potlitical grass leaves movement—a cross-fertilization of the hippie and New Left philosophies.
2. A connecting link that would tie together as much of the underground as was willing into some gigantic national get-together.
3. The development of a model for an alternative society.
4. The need to make some statement, especially in revolutionary action-theater terms, about LBJ, the Democratic Party, electoral politics, and the state of the nation.

To accomplish these tasks required the construction of a vast myth, for through the notion of myth large numbers of people could get turned on and, in that process of getting turned on, begin to participate in Yippie! and start to focus on Chicago. *Precision was sacrificed for a greater degree of suggestion.* People took off in all directions in the most sensational manner possible:

"We will burn Chicago to the ground!"

"We will fuck on the beaches!"

"We demand the Politics of Ecstasy!"

"Acid for all!"

"Abandon the Creeping Meatball!"

And all the time: "Yippie! Chicago — August 25-30."

Reporters would play their preconceived roles: "What is the difference between a hippie and a Yippie?" A hundred different answers would fly out, forcing the reporter to make up his own answers; to distort. And distortion became the life-blood of the Yippies.

Yippie! was in the eye of the beholder. . . .

From *Revolution for the Hell of It* by Abbie Hoffman. The Dial Press, Inc., 1968.

A Constitutional Convention is being planned. A convention of visionary mind-benders who will for five long days and nights address themselves to the task of formulating the goals and means of the New Society.

It will be a blend of technologists and poets, of artists and community organizers, of anyone who has a vision. We will try to develop a Community of Consciousness.

There will be a huge rock-folk festival for free. Contrary to rumor, no groups originally committed to Chicago have dropped out. In fact, additional ones have agreed to participate. In all about thirty groups and performers will be there.

Theater groups from all over the country are pledged to come. They are an integral part of the activities, and a large amount of funds raised from here on in will go for the transportation of street theater groups.

Workshops in a variety of subjects such as draft resistance, drugs, commune development, guerrilla theater and under-ground media will be set up. The workshops will be oriented around problem-solving while the Constitutional Convention works to developing the overall philosophical framework.

There will probably be a huge march across town to haunt the Democrats.

People coming to Chicago should begin preparations for five days of energy-exchange. Do not come prepared to sit and watch and be fed and cared for. It just won't happen that way. It is time to become a life-actor. The days of the audience died with the old America. If you don't have a thing to do, stay home, you'll only get in the way. . . .

We are negotiating, with the Chicago city government, a six-day treaty. . . . We have had several meetings, principally with David Stahl, Deputy Mayor of Chicago, and there remains but to iron out the terms of the treaty—suspension of curfew laws, regulations pertaining to sleeping on the beach, etc.—for us to have a bona fide permit in our hands.

The possibility of violence will be greatly reduced. There is no guarantee that it will be entirely eliminated.

This is the United States, 1968, remember. If you are afraid of violence you shouldn't have crossed the border.

This matter of a permit is a cat-and-mouse game. The Chicago authorities do not wish to grant it too early, knowing this would increase the number of people that descend on the city. They can ill afford to wait too late, for that will inhibit planning on our part and create more chaos.

It is not our wish to take on superior armed troops who outnumber us on unfamiliar enemy territory. It is not their wish to have a Democrat nominated amidst a major bloodbath. The treaty will work for both sides. . . .

Prepare a street theater skit or bring something to distribute, such as food, poems or music. Get sleeping bags and other camping equipment. . . .

The point is, you can use Chicago as a means of pulling your local community together. It can serve to open up a dialogue between political radicals and those who might be considered hippies. The radical will say to the hippie: "Get together and fight, you are getting the shit kicked out of you." The hippie will say to the radical: "Your protest is so narrow, your rhetoric so boring, your ideological power plays so old-fashioned."

Each can help the other, and Chicago . . . might well offer the medium to put forth that message.

Counter Culture

Some of those who participated in the New Left and the "counter culture" did so as an expression of their thorough disgust with American society. They became increasingly infatuated with Third World liberation struggles and made heroes of revolutionaries like Che Guevara and Mao Zedong. Many, however, had a much more ambivalent relationship to American culture. Indeed, at some level the "counter culture" can be seen as part of a deep strain in American culture that has always valued personal expression over conformity.

This short poem by Jerry Rubin captures this ambivalence. Rubin, a cofounder of the Yippies!, was certainly seen by the public as one of those who disliked what America stood for and advocated its destruction, yet his writing reveals him to be very much in love with American culture despite the alienation he feels because of its corruption. Excerpted from Jerry Rubin, Do It! Scenarios of the Revolution *(New York, 1970), 12-13.*

Child of Amerika

I am a child of Amerika.

If I'm ever sent to Death Row for my revolutionary "crimes," I'll order as my last meal: a hamburger, french fries and a Coke.

I dig big cities.

I love to read the sports pages and gossip columns, listen to the radio and watch color TV.

I dig department stores, huge supermarkets and airports. I feel secure (though not necessarily hungry) when I see Howard Johnson's on the expressway.

I groove on Hollywood movies—even bad ones.

I speak only one language—English.

I love rock 'n' roll.

San Francisco's Haight-Ashbury became one center of America's counter culture. Some came looking for an alternative to a sterile, consumer-based society, others merely looked for sex, drugs and rock and roll. (Courtesy of AP/Wide World Photos.)

I collected baseball players' cards when I was a kid and wanted to play second base for the Cincinnati Reds, my home team.

I got a car when I was sixteen after flunking my first driver's test and crying for a week waiting to take it a second time.

I went to the kind of high school where you had to pass a test to get *in*.

I graduated in the bottom half of the class.

Reprinted with the permission of Simon & Schuster from *DO IT! Scenarios of the Revolution* by Jerry Rubin. Copyright © 1970 by Social Education Foundation.

My classmates voted me the "busiest" senior in the school.
I had short, short, short hair.
I dug *Catcher in the Rye*.
I didn't have pimples.

I became an ace young reporter for the Cincinnati *Post and Times-Star*. "*Son*," the managing editor said to me, "*someday you're going to be a helluva reporter, maybe the greatest reporter this city's ever seen.*"
I loved Adlai Stevenson.
My father drove a truck delivering bread and later became an organizer in the Bakery Drivers' Union. He dug Jimmy Hoffa (so do I). He died of heart failure at fifty-two.
My mother had a college degree and played the piano. She died of cancer at the age of fifty-one.
I took care of my brother, Gil, from the time he was thirteen.
I dodged the draft.
I went to Oberlin College for a year, graduated from the University of Cincinnati, spent 1 1/2 years in Israel and started graduate school at Berkeley.
I dropped out.
I dropped out of the White Race and the Amerikan nation.
I dig being free.
I like getting high.
I don't own a suit or tie.
I live for the revolution.
I'm a yippie!
I am an orphan of Amerika.

Communes and Alternative Living

The "counter culture" also found some of its members among those for whom New Left politics and the civil rights and anti-war movements had become equally corrupt power struggles. Raymond Mungo was such a wounded veteran of the movement. As the Yippies! prepared to go to Chicago in 1968, Mungo embarked on a personal odyssey that landed him at Total Loss Farm, a commune in Vermont.

*Mungo, and others like him, retreated from the chaotic, and ulti-
mately futile, world of opposition politics to experiment with alternative
ways of living. Often these experiments embraced a "back to the land"
philosophy that manifested itself in the creation of primitive rural communities. Mungo turned his back on American society, but he did so in a
thoroughly American way. His experiences, and the book from which this
selection is taken, were clearly inspired by the journeys of Beat generation author Jack Kerouac and the descent of Henry David Thoreau.
Taken from Raymond Mungo,* Total Loss Farm: A Year in the Life
(New York, 1970), 16-17, 133, 157-59.

When we lived in Boston, Chicago, San Francisco, Washington (you name it, we lived there; some of us still live there), we
dreamed of a New Age born of violent insurrection. We danced
on the graves of war dead in Vietnam, every corpse was ammunition for Our Side; we set up a countergovernment down there in
Washington, had marches, rallies and meetings; tried to fight fire
with fire. Then Johnson resigned, yes, and the universities began
to fall, the best and the oldest ones first, and by God every 13-year-
old in the suburbs was smoking dope and our numbers multiply-
ing into the millions. But I woke up in the spring of 1968 and said,
"This is not what I had in mind," because the movement had
become my enemy; the movement was not flowers and doves and
spontaneity, but another vicious system, the seed of a heartless
bureaucracy, a minority Party vying for power rather than peace.
It was then that we put away the schedule for the revolution,
gathered together our dear ones and all our resources, and set off
to Vermont in search of the New Age.

The New Age we were looking for proved to be very old
indeed, and I've often wondered aloud at my luck for being 23
years old in a time and place in which only the past offers hope
and inspiration; the future offers only artifice and blight. I travel
now in a society of friends who heat their houses with hand-cut
wood and eliminate in outhouses, who cut pine shingles with
draw-knives and haul maple sugar sap on sleds, who weed pota-
toes with their university-trained hands, pushing long hair out of
their way and thus marking their foreheads with beautiful peni-
tent dust. We till the soil to atone for our fathers' destruction of it.

We smell. We live far from the marketplaces in America by our own volition, and the powerful men left behind are happy to have us out of their way. They do not yet realize that their heirs will refuse to inhabit their hollow cities, will find them poisonous and lethal, will run back to the Stone Age if necessary for survival and peace. . . .

Over the crest of the hill, for the first time the road descends—walking downhill for a stretch we can catch our breath. That's why we built the road so, that horses pulling loads up the farm could recuperate from the uphill struggle and, freshened, go on. The road dips down to a wooden bridge crossing a stream of many colors in which pickerel, trout, salmon, tuna, and whales have been spotted by the sharpest of eyes. Most folks see only an occasional small trout or sunfish in this Noname Brook, which leads nowhere, but that is because they are all nearsighted. They wear glasses in the faith that the real, or actual, universe is not the one their own eyes can see, but a standard, universal universe dictated by prescription, or politics. You'd certainly be welcome to hang on to your specs here, but this is a place where you *could* take them off without fear of ridicule or violence to your body. Without my glasses, the brook becomes a dazzling pulsating streak of sunlight across the earth, ill-defined and like the great Source difficult to watch for long. They say it can blind you, but how to know which things you might better be blind to? Our great adventure after all is in searching for something not only better but new, nothing less than the next step in the evolution of the race, which may be somewhere we've been before. It goes in spells. And in racing toward the New Age, we can't be expected to carry all the dead weight of the past—all the schools, factories, newspapers, jobs, religions, and movements—which would drag us under. Just do whatever comes to mind, do something you hadn't thought of before, it's bound to get you *somewhere*. And you'll then decide whether you like it and where to move on to. We might stay at the brook all day and be perfectly happy, even dangle our toes in the chilly clear water, but me I'm now anxious to get on up to the farm. Coming? . . .

We *are* saving the world, of course, as the world for us extends to the boundaries of Total Loss Farm and the limits of our own experience; and Total Loss Farm is everywhere now, perhaps under your own rhubarb patch if you looked at it a little closer, and our experience all that anyone could hope to know of life. We were born and raised by parents who loved us at least until they lost us to a certain high-pitched whistle in the wind which they had gotten too old to hear; we work at maintaining ourselves, though our shared labor is seldom very taxing, for it takes little enough work to make plants grow, most of it is out of our hands, and our relationship to the work one of direct gratification and reward, as children insist on; we have children of our own, though they are fully peers by the time they've learned to eat and eliminate without physical help, and soon become more our masters than our students; and we die, sometimes in sulphurous flames, dramatic and shocking, other times silent and mysterious like the gone children wandering Europe with scenes of the parents engulfed in atrocity scrawled across their minds, but never to be spoken: "I come from Auschwitz, or Hué, or Boston, my father was shot for believing in God and hangs limp forever in front of our home as a reminder to the others; my mother was sold to the grim green soldiers for their sport, my brother to be used as a woman; I escaped the country of the somnambulent and blind on the back of a wolf who prowled the ruins and took pity on me; I have come here to begin again."

Our parents must wonder where we are, this story is, as much as anything else, an attempt to fill them in, but it grows harder and harder to speak. Fortunately, it grows simultaneously less necessary. I have clothes on my back, though they are old, and a roof over my head and food for my belly. In this, I am luckier than many. I am surrounded by people who would give their own lives in defense of mine, for they know we will make it together or not at all. I wish to be reconciled with all of my enemies, and to live on the planet and glory in peaches to a ripe old age. I am willing to help you as much as I'm able, as a single person can help another, not as a movement or government can help a mass. I may ask for some help from you as well. If you come to my house with love in your heart and there's room for one more—for there isn't always—you may know I will feed you and house you for the night, if you need it. You may see me walking from town to town with my thumb outstretched to the highway, seeking a lift: don't pass me by.

You have seen me everywhere. I am not asking for the vote. I do not seek to be represented. I do not seek to tear down your buildings or march on your castle or sit at your desk. I am interested neither in destroying what you have put up nor in gaining control of your empire. I demand nothing, and nothing is my inheritance. I live in the world, in the woods, with my friends, where not many people come by and the planet is entire and friendly; we like to be left alone except by those who can help. You can help by giving the planet, and peace, a chance. I ask only that you treat yourself right, give yourself the best of everything; and in so doing, you will be acting for me as well. If you can't stop, at least wave as you go by. Slow down, perhaps stop working: you'll find the time for everything you really want to do.

The "Silent Majority" Responds

In the autumn of 1969 President Richard Nixon, in a nationally televised address, contrasted what he believed to be a minority of Americans engaging in disruptive protest, with what he called "the silent majority"— suburban, law-abiding, conservative, middle-class citizens. It was this majority whose opinion Nixon courted in dealing with protesters and the "counter culture."

Promising to bring the nation together, and heal its wounds, Nixon often tried to play the elder statesman when he publicly discussed demonstrators, leaving it to his vice president, Spiro Agnew, to set a more strident and bellicose tone against protesters. Agnew was surely given this assignment by Nixon, who we now know was enraged at student demonstrators who challenged his policies. Asked by a reporter whether his aggressive posturing differed from the president's attitude, Vice President Agnew responded: "When the president said 'bring us together' he meant the functioning, contributing portions of the American citizenry."

In the speech excerpted below, Agnew calls for a "positive polarization" of the American public. It is an extraordinary gesture for a vice president to announce division as official government policy, but such was the nature of the Nixon administration. Nearly three decades later Agnew's demands for "law and order" strike us as richly ironic. Spiro Agnew was forced to resign for taking bribes, and Nixon, the great champion of law and order, came to think of impeachment before resigning in disgrace because of the Watergate scandal. Taken from Spiro T. Agnew, Frankly Speaking: A Collection of Extraordinary Speeches *(Washington, 1970), 44-49, 51.*

What I said before, I will say again. It is time for the preponderant majority, the responsible citizens of this country, to assert *their* rights. It is time to stop dignifying the immature actions of arrogant, reckless, inexperienced elements within our society. The reason is compelling. It is simply that their tantrums are insidiously destroying the fabric of American democracy. . . .

Last week I was lambasted for my lack of "mental and moral sensitivity." I say that any leader who does not perceive where persistent street struggles are going to lead this nation lacks mental acuity. And any leader who does not caution this nation on the danger of this direction lacks moral strength.

I believe in Constitutional dissent. I believe in the people registering their views with their elected representatives, and I commend those people who care enough about their country to involve themselves in its great issues. I believe in legal protest within the Constitutional limits of free speech, including peaceful assembly and the right of petition. But I do not believe that demonstrations, lawful or unlawful, merit my approval or even my silence where the purpose is fundamentally unsound. In the case of the Vietnam Moratorium [15 October 1969, a day of demonstrations, actions, vigils, and petition drives across the nation], the objective announced by the leaders—immediate unilateral withdrawal of all our forces from Vietnam—was not only unsound but idiotic. The tragedy was that thousands who participated wanted only to show a fervent desire for peace, but were used by the political hustlers who ran the event. . . .

Think about it. Small bands of students are allowed to shut down great universities. Small groups of dissidents are allowed to shout down political candidates. Small cadres of professional protestors are allowed to jeopardize the peace efforts of the President of the United States.

It is time to question the credentials of their leaders. And, if in questioning we disturb a few people, I say it is time for them to be disturbed. If, in challenging, we polarize the American people, I say it is time for a positive polarization.

It is time for a healthy in-depth examination of policies and a constructive realignment in this country. It is time to rip away the rhetoric and to divide on authentic lines. It is time to discard the fiction that in a country of 200 million people, everyone is qualified to quarterback the government. . . .

Now, we have among us a glib, activist element who would tell us our values are lies, and I call them impudent. Because anyone who impugns a legacy of liberty and dignity that reaches back to Moses, is impudent.

I call them snobs for most of them disdain to mingle with the masses who work for a living. They mock the common man's pride in his work, his family and his country. It has also been said that I called them intellectuals. I did not. I said that they characterized themselves as intellectuals. No true intellectual, no truly knowledgeable person, would so despise democratic institutions.

America cannot afford to write off a whole generation for the decadent thinking of a few. America cannot afford to divide over their demagoguery, to be deceived by their duplicity, or to let their license destroy liberty. We can, however, afford to separate them from our society—with no more regret than we should feel over discarding rotten apples from a barrel. . . .

. . . [I]t is time to stop demonstrating in the streets and start doing something constructive about our institutions. America must recognize the dangers of constant carnival. Americans must reckon with irresponsible leadership and reckless words. The mature and sensitive people of this country must realize that their freedom of protest is being exploited by avowed anarchists and communists who detest everything about this country and want to destroy it. . . .

Will we defend fifty centuries of accumulated wisdom? For that is our heritage. Will we make the effort to preserve America's bold, successful experiment in truly representative government? Or do we care so little that we will cast it all aside?

Questions

---

1. *Compare and contrast the "three streams" of dissent.*
2. *To what extent did "culture" play a role in these movements? Can cultural rebellion be the same thing as political rebellion? Why or why not?*
3. *What is the role of violence, or the threat of violence, for each of these groups?*
4. *What is the legacy of each "stream" today?*

FURTHER READING

For the most complete accounts of SDS and related movements, see Todd Gitlin, The Sixties: Years of Hope, Days of Rage *(New York, 1987) and James Miller,* "Democracy is in the Streets": From Port Huron to The Siege of Chicago *(New York, 1987). Stewart Burns's* Social Movements of the 1960s: Searching for Democracy *(Boston, 1990) provides a largely sympathetic survey of these movements. One of the best studies of SNCC remains Carson Clayborne,* In Struggle: SNCC and the Black Awakening of the 1960s *(Cambridge, Massachusetts, 1981). Perhaps the most insightful, best-written analysis of the relationship between protest movements and the Nixon administration is Jonathan Schell's* The Time of Illusion *(New York, 1975). For the best contextualization of the drama of the 1960s see Godfrey Hodgson's* America in Our Time *(New York, 1976).*

Why Did
the United States
Lose the Vietnam War?

Mark Grimsley

INTRODUCTION

Ordered to return to Southeast Asia at the beginning of Rambo: First Blood Part II *(1985), the title character caustically inquires, "Do we get to win this time?" The premise of the film, and a raft of others like it, was that the United States betrayed the soldiers it sent to fight in Vietnam—in part because the U.S. government allegedly abandoned POWs and MIAs it knew were being held after the war's end (Rambo's mission is to retrieve them), but more fundamentally because the American military could have won the war if only the American government and people had let them. The fictional Rambo's bitterness reflects a very real bitterness among certain segments of American society. Equally bitter are those who believe that the United States could not possibly have won the war at reasonable cost, and therefore should not have intervened in the first place. Thus, the question, "Why did the United States lose the Vietnam War?" is possibly the most divisive issue in recent American history.*

The United States plainly lost the war in the sense that it committed its armed might and prestige to a venture that ultimately failed. But in an important sense—as people on both sides of the issue acknowledge—the United States could not have "won" the Vietnam War. Only the South Vietnamese government could do that. From the first, American policy in Vietnam was designed to assist the South Vietnamese toward that end. The difficulty lies in assessing the extent to which that policy succeeded—or might have succeeded—in helping the South Vietnamese regime prevail against its Communist rivals, the North Vietnamese and the Viet Cong.

212

Both North and South Vietnam were barely a decade old when the first American combat troops splashed ashore in 1965. Before 1954, Vietnam had been part of French Indochina, a colony that also included present-day Laos and Cambodia. France's defeat by the Germans in 1940 had allowed the Japanese to occupy Indochina during World War II. After Japan's defeat in 1945, the French had returned to find that Vietnamese nationalists, led by Ho Chi Minh, now sought complete independence from any foreign power. A long, bitter guerrilla war began soon thereafter. Because Ho Chi Minh and his followers were avowed Communists, the United States supported the French with money and equipment. After a stunning defeat in 1954 led the French to abandon Indochina, the United States was party to an agreement whereby Vietnam was divided at the 17th parallel into two parts—North Vietnam, controlled by the Communists, and South Vietnam, controlled by Ngo Dinh Diem, a ruler friendly to the United States but only weakly supported by the South Vietnamese people.

In 1961, the Communist North Vietnamese organized the National Liberation Front, composed of South Vietnamese who wished to defeat the Diem regime and unite with North Vietnam. Dubbed the "Viet Cong"—short for Vietnamese Communists— the National Liberation Front soon began a guerrilla war against the Diem regime, supported directly by North Vietnam and indirectly by the Soviet Union and Communist China. The John F. Kennedy administration regarded South Vietnam as a bulwark against communism in Southeast Asia and supported the South Vietnamese government with money, equipment, and military advisers. By 1963, however, it was clear that the Diem regime was too inept to defeat the Viet Cong. Hoping that new leadership might improve the situation, the U.S. government approved a military coup in which Diem was killed. When the situation in South Vietnam continued to decline, Kennedy's successor, Lyndon B. Johnson, began bombing attacks against North Vietnam in August 1964, followed by the commitment of ground troops in early 1965.

By deploying American armed forces directly, the Johnson administration believed it could force the North Vietnamese and

Viet Cong to desist from further aggression against South Vietnam. But the Johnson administration deliberately chose to conduct the war in a limited fashion, fearing that unrestricted bombing or an invasion of North Vietnam risked intervention by the Communist Chinese (as had occurred during the Korean War). The Johnson administration also feared that a full military mobilization would undercut its ambitious domestic spending program, the Great Society. But surely, it was thought, complete military mobilization was unnecessary to defeat a small Third World nation. A Marine lieutenant sent to Vietnam spoke for many Americans when he remarked, "[W]e carried, along with our packs and rifles, the implicit conviction that the Viet Cong would be quickly beaten."

Eight years later, in 1973, after losing more than fifty-eight thousand American lives, the United States withdrew from South Vietnam. The South Vietnamese regime fell to a final North Vietnamese invasion in 1975. What happened?

THE TURNING POINT: TET 1968

Until early 1968, Americans were told—and most believed—that the United States was winning the war in Vietnam. Although this reflected the sincere opinions of many U.S. policymakers, it also was due to a deliberately orchestrated public relations campaign of "accentuating the positive." In their public pronouncements, American officials emphasized U.S. and South Vietnamese successes, while carefully downplaying elements that suggested a bleaker picture.

Then, on 31 January 1968, the North Vietnamese and Viet Cong launched surprise attacks all over South Vietnam, striking at over a hundred cities and towns, including the capital city of Saigon itself. Timed to take advantage of a temporary truce in observance of the Lunar New Year—"Tet"—this massive wave of attacks at once became known as the Tet Offensive. Historians agree that it was a major turning point in America's involvement in Vietnam.

It would be wrong to say that, prior to Tet, most Americans were enthusiastic about the war. A poll taken in November 1967 revealed that 44 percent of Americans favored a gradual or total withdrawal from Vietnam, while another 55 percent believed the United States should pursue a more vigorous policy. But the Tet Offensive greatly intensified doubts that the United States could defeat the Communists within an acceptable time frame and at an acceptable cost. This was not because the Tet Offensive was a victory for North Vietnamese and Viet Cong forces. On the contrary, in purely military terms it was a Communist disaster. Gen. William C. Westmoreland, the commander of U.S. forces in Vietnam, estimated that as many as fifty thousand North Vietnamese and Viet Cong soldiers were killed. Yet two thousand Americans (and four thousand South Vietnamese soldiers, as well as over twelve thousand South Vietnamese civilians) also perished—a staggering casualty list that made a hollow boast of predictions that the war could be won within a year or two. Respected and influential television journalist Walter Cronkite captured the mood of many Americans in the wake of Tet: "To

*say that we are mired in stalemate seems the only reasonable, yet unsat-
isfactory conclusion."*

*The following excerpts portray the shock of the Tet Offensive, its
impact on American public opinion and policymakers, and the shift in
U.S. policy it generated.*

The Attack on the U.S. Embassy

---

*The initial phase of the Tet Offensive included a strike against the U.S.
Embassy in Saigon. Militarily it was—as one American officer said
dismissively—"a piddling platoon action," but politically it was stunning. If the huge American military presence in South Vietnam could
not prevent Viet Cong commandos from storming the U.S. Embassy, the
feeling went, how could it possibly be achieving the success that American generals and officials were promising?*

*American journalist Don Oberdorfer drew on dozens of personal
interviews as well as official sources for his account of the Tet Offensive,
published in 1971. Here he describes the embassy attack. Excerpted from
Don Oberdorfer,* Tet! *(1971; reprint ed., New York, 1984), 6–8, 28.*

On a Saigon street corner just before midnight, a wiry, muscu-
lar man named Nguyen Van Sau kept a rendezvous with an
officer of the Viet Cong C-10 Battalion. Sau was a squad leader
normally stationed at battalion base headquarters, which was
near the Michelin Rubber Plantation only thirty miles north of the
capital. He came to the site of the battle the day before not as a
soldier in formation, but as an ordinary civilian on the back of a
commercial truck on a main highway—just one more traveling
celebrant of the national festival of Tet.

Like many soldiers of the revolution, Sau had been an illiter-
ate farmer when he was recruited for the cause. Born in a village
on the outskirts of Saigon, he attended only one year of school
before going to work in the rice fields. He joined the Liberation

Army [the Viet Cong] in 1964. . . . When the C-10 battalion was established for sapper [a term, normally used to describe a combat engineer, but used by the Viet Cong to mean a commando-raider] and sabotage activities in the Saigon area in late 1965, Sau was assigned to the unit. In 1966 he was promoted to squad leader and in March of 1967 he was permitted to join the People's Revolutionary Party, the Communist Party of South Vietnam.

In November of 1967—three months prior to Tet—Sau's section of the C-10 Battalion began to ship ammunition and explosives to Saigon from a supply cache at headquarters. The first shipment of ammunition and TNT [explosive] moved in a rented truck piled high with firewood. Three other shipments were concealed in large baskets of tomatoes which came into the city down Route 1.

Two days before Tet, big and unusually heavy baskets of "tomatoes" and large bamboo containers of "rice" were moved to a house adjoining the small automobile repair shop at 59 Phan Thanh Gian Street. The house and garage were owned by Mrs. Nguyen Thi Phe, who had been working for the Viet Cong in Saigon for thirteen years and had been arrested several times for subversive activities.

Shortly after midnight on Tet night, sapper Sau and the other members of the team assembled at the garage. The shipments of weapons were broken out and distributed, and the soldiers briefed for the first time on their combat mission. It is probable that most of them, including Sau, had barely heard of the United States Embassy and had little understanding of the significance of their mission that night. Sau did not learn what he was supposed to do after penetrating the exterior wall of the Embassy compound. Nothing was said about replacements or an escape route, but there is no indication the soldiers were told this was a suicide raid.

At 2:45 A.M. they were rolling through the streets toward the Embassy in a small Peugeot truck and a taxicab. . . . The truck and taxi turned the corner onto Thong Nhut (Reunification) Boulevard, a broad, tree-lined avenue dominated on one side by the eight-foot outer wall of the American Embassy compound. As the taxicab rounded the corner, its passengers opened fire with automatic weapons at the two MPs [military policemen] standing just outside the night gate of the Embassy on the side street. The small truck stopped on the boulevard side of the high compound wall.

American soldiers guard the U.S. embassy building in Saigon after its attack by Viet Cong snappers during the Tet Offensive. News of the attack shocked the American home front, exploding the myth that the United States was on the brink of victory in Vietnam. (Courtesy of Dick Swanson/ Life Magazine © Time, Inc.)

The men, wearing neckerchiefs and arm bands for identification, climbed out and quickly began unloading rockets and explosive charges.

Specialist Fourth Class Charles L. Daniel, twenty-three, of Durham, North Carolina, and Private First Class William E. Sebast, twenty, of Albany, New York, fired back at the taxicab, then moved inside. They slammed the steel gate and locked it with a heavy padlock and chain. At 2:47 A.M. they radioed "Signal 300"—MP brevity code for enemy attack.

A moment later an explosion rocked the compound. With a flash and a blast, a fifteen-pound explosive charge blew a three-foot hole in the high wall of the compound near the corner where the truck had stopped.

Daniel and Sebast wheeled around and began firing at the invaders scrambling through the hole. Daniel shouted into the MP radio: "They're coming in! They're coming in! Help me! Help me!" Then the radio went dead. Daniel's body was found later with bullet wounds in the head; Sebast had been shot through the chest. From the positions of their bodies and the bullet holes in the wall behind them, it appeared they were facing the invaders when they died. It is likely that their first shots killed the two Viet Cong leaders, the first men through the hole in the wall.

A Military Police jeep patrol cruising several blocks away heard the call for help and responded immediately. Sergeant Jonnie B. Thomas, twenty-four, of Detroit, and Specialist Fourth Class Owen E. Mebust, twenty, of Lynwood, California, sped down the boulevard toward the Embassy. They were met by a hail of automatic weapons fire. Thomas and Mebust were the third and fourth Americans to be killed at the Embassy in the first five minutes.

U.S. Public Learns of Attack

The first news reports of the attack on the Embassy flashed worldwide barely fifteen minutes after it began. An Associated Press correspondent wired a steady stream of updates by teletype. His reports reached New York just as the major television networks were about to air their evening news programs. Here is the lead story that night as broadcast by NBC anchorman Chet Huntley:

The Vietcong seized part of the U.S. Embassy in Saigon early Wednesday, Vietnam time. Snipers are in the buildings and on roof tops near the Embassy and are firing on American personnel inside the compound.

Twenty suicide commandos are reported to be holding the first floor of the Embassy.

The attack on the Embassy and other key installations in Saigon, at Tan Son Nhut Air Base and Bien Hoa north of Saigon came as the climax of the enemy's biggest and most highly coordinated offensive of the war. There was no report on Allied casualties in Saigon, but they're believed to be high.

In the Vietnam War, stunning images like this one frequently undercut a more nuanced view of the conflict. Here South Vietnam's National Police Chief summarily executes a Viet Cong officer in the early days of the Tet Offensive. This image horrified the American public; few learned the officer had been captured after murdering several civilian hostages, including a mother and her children. (Photograph by Eddie Adams. Courtesy of AP/Wide World Photos.)

The attacks came as thousands of civilians were celebrating the Lunar New Year, and at times it was almost impossible to distinguish the explosion of mortar shells and small arms fire from those of the firecrackers the celebrants were setting off.

General Westmoreland Reacts

Although surprised by the scope and ferocity of the Tet Offensive, Gen. Westmoreland, the commander of MACV (Military Assistance Command, Vietnam), regarded it with some reason as a major Communist miscalculation and a potential U.S. opportunity. As for the attack on the embassy, to him it was tactically insignificant, virtually a blip on the screen. He was therefore somewhat surprised that the White House seemed inordinately concerned about it, and even more so when he arrived at the embassy shortly after its recapture by U.S. troops—an event that occurred barely six hours after Sau and his comrades first entered the compound. Taken from William C. Westmoreland, A Soldier Reports, *(Garden City, New York, 1976), 324–25.*

With the coming of daylight a platoon of U.S. airborne troops landed on the helicopter pad on the roof of the Chancery [the main embassy building], but by that time the fight was over. All fifteen VC sappers were dead, along with the five Americans and four Vietnamese employees of the Embassy, one of whom may have been a VC collaborator.

As soon as I learned that the airborne troops had landed, I drove by car to the Embassy. It was about 8:30 A.M. Like any battlefield, the compound was in disarray, bodies of Americans and Vietnamese still lying about. Yet unlike most battlefields, American reporters and television cameramen were seemingly everywhere. Their faces mirrored dismay and incredulity, as if the end of the world was at hand.

. . . [I was asked] to hold a press conference on the scene. I took the opportunity to try to put the Embassy raid and the country-side attacks into perspective.

Contrary to rumor, I said, none of the Viet Cong had gotten inside the Chancery. Damage to the building was superficial. As for the big offensive throughout the country, the enemy, by coming into the open, was exposing himself to tremendous casualties. Fully conscious of American and South Vietnamese strength and ability, I had no hesitation in saying that the enemy was inviting defeat.

My efforts at perspective went for nought. The attack on the Embassy, [journalist] Don Oberdorfer wrote later, "seemed to give the lie to the rosy projections and victory claims that Westmoreland and others had been dishing out." Oberdorfer said that the reporters could hardly believe their ears. "Westmoreland was standing in the ruins and saying everything was great."

Excerpts from "The Tet Offensive" reprinted from *A Soldier Reports* by General William C. Westmoreland, published by Doubleday & Company, Inc., 1976. Copyright © 1976 by William C. Westmoreland.

That attitude on the part of the American reporters undoubtedly contributed to the psychological victory the enemy achieved in the United States. What would they have had me say, that the walls were tumbling down when I knew they were not? That the enemy was winning when I knew he was on the verge of a disastrous military defeat? . . .

In the race to drain every possible sensation from the Embassy story, reporters made little apparent effort to check facts. . . . Chet Huntley on the NBC Evening News had the VC inside the Chancery, the defenders in the compound outside. There was no report on Allied casualties in Saigon, said Huntley, "but they're believed to be high." Was that kind of gratuitous speculation justified? Was the long, costly American effort in Vietnam to be sacrificed to the idols of sensation and competition?

A Reporter's View

Peter Braestrup was the Saigon bureau chief for the Washington Post at the time of the Tet Offensive. In later years he wrote a study of news coverage during the offensive that echoed the criticisms made by Westmoreland. "[M]any of these reporters," Braestrup acknowledged, "were inexperienced in military operations or in the tactics of the Communists. Particularly the television people had no real grip on the football game. They could go out and take pictures of the players and the drama. But they were like sportswriters who had no concept of the game they were covering." Even so, Braestrup rejected the view that the media was the primary culprit in shaping the myth that Tet was a military disaster for the Americans and South Vietnamese. Abridged from Al Santoli, To Bear Any Burden: The Vietnam War and Its Aftermath in the Words of Americans and Southeast Asians, *(New York, 1985), 180–81.*

The press, in terms of themes they convey, are a reflective institution. They have cultural biases and there are trends and fashions. But on the big issues, the president of the United States dominates when he wants to. Why did the media press the panic button at Tet? President Lyndon Johnson seemed to have been struck by a kind of immobility. . . .

Johnson knew that something big was coming because General Westmoreland had told him. He had sent reinforcements ahead of time—the 11th Infantry Brigade from Hawaii and two brigades of the 101st Airborne.

But Johnson never mentioned this in his State of the Union Address [just prior to the Tet Offensive]. He was doing everything possible to downplay the idea of war—and, with an election year in progress, upgrade the idea of peace negotiations. So he failed to prepare the public or the press.

From the start, the President had failed to define a clear strategy for winning the war. He failed to mobilize the country or decide how we were going to end the war. He was grasping for straws and buying time, hoping something would turn up. Public opinion—the man on the street—doesn't quite know what's going on, but he's not satisfied with this. So Lyndon brought home the famous "progress campaign" of 1967. Everybody was brought in from Vietnam, including General Westmoreland, to say, "We're making progress." That was short-term relief in the Gallup polls for Lyndon. Then comes Tet.

All of a sudden, everybody is saying, "We can't go on like this." The hawks are saying it behind closed doors, the doves are saying it out loud. And Johnson isn't saying anything. For two months he doesn't say anything and takes no decisive action. He did not do what Richard Nixon did in the 1972 election year—send in the B-52s and mine Haiphong Harbor—take a forceful retaliatory posture against the North Vietnamese. Nixon's popularity went up. And though he wasn't popular with the press, his policy was coherent. They understood that he had a scenario. He did not leave a vacuum. He was a decisive, forceful president in a time of crisis. That is what the public looks to. And that is what the press looks to also.

At Tet, Lyndon Johnson in effect got into his bunker. He left the political debate and furor in the hands of his critics and to the press. Johnson was in a crisis of his own making. The press will aggravate any president's problems. If the President is nervous or indecisive, the press will make it worse. And more of his critics will come out of the woodwork.

Excerpts from "Grasping Straws" by Peter Braestrup, as it appeared in *To Bear Any Burden: The Vietnam War and Its Aftermath in the Words of Americans and Southeast Asians,* published by E.P. Dutton, 1985. Copyright © 1985 by Al Santoli.

The press, in effect, becomes a prism. Concentrating the heat on the White House. But the President starts the demoralization himself. He's like the platoon leader. If they run into an ambush, all the troops look to the platoon leader to take charge. If he's lying on the ground for ten, twenty, a hundred seconds, the troops get demoralized himself. That's what happened at Tet. One trooper, like Walter Cronkite, who's a little shook, will say, "Let's get the hell out of here." Panic will start. And the press will overreact to everything. That's the way they are.

Questions in the Wake of Tet

In fact, President Lyndon B. Johnson briefly wanted to redouble the American military effort after Tet, as Gen. Westmoreland advised. But many of his advisers had doubts, among them, newly-appointed Secretary of Defense Clark Clifford. Clifford replaced Robert S. McNamara, who had quietly resigned the office because of misgivings about American policy in Vietnam (policy he had done as much as anyone to create). Clifford soon had misgivings of his own. Taken from Clark M. Clifford, "A Viet Nam Reappraisal: The Personal History of One Man's View and How It Evolved," Foreign Affairs *47 (July 1969): 609–13.*

I took office on March 1, 1968. The enemy's Tet offensive of late January and early February had been beaten back at great cost. The confidence of the American people had been badly shaken. The ability of the South Vietnamese Government to restore order and morale in the populace, and discipline and esprit in the armed forces, was being questioned. At the President's direction, General Earle G. Wheeler, Chairman of the Joint Chiefs of Staff, had flown to Viet Nam in late February for an on-the-spot conference with General Westmoreland. He had just returned and presented the military's request that over 200,000 troops be pre-

---

pared for deployment to Viet Nam. These troops would be in addition to the 525,000 previously authorized. I was directed, as my first assignment, to chair a task force named by the President to determine how this new requirement could be met. We were not instructed to assess the need for substantial increases in men and matériel; we were to devise the means by which they could be provided. . . . Try though we would to stay with the assignment of devising means to meet the military's requests, fundamental questions began to recur over and over.

. . . [H]ere are some of the principal issues raised and some of the answers as I understood them:

"Will 200,000 more men do the job?" I found no assurance that they would.

"If not, how many more might be needed—and when?" There was no way of knowing.

"What would be involved in committing 200,000 more men to Viet Nam?" A reserve call-up of approximately 280,000, an increased draft call and an extension of tours of duty of most men then in service.

"Can the enemy respond with a build-up of his own?" He could and he probably would.

"What are the estimated costs of the latest requests?" First calculations were on the order of $2 billion for the remaining four months of that fiscal year, and an increase of $10 to $12 billion for the year beginning July 1, 1968.

"What will be the impact on the economy?" So great that we would face the possibility of credit restrictions, a tax increase and even wage and price controls. The balance of payments would be worsened by at least half a billion dollars a year.

"Can bombing stop the war?" Never by itself. It was inflicting heavy personnel and matériel losses, but bombing by itself would not stop the war.

"Will stepping up the bombing decrease American casualties?" Very little, if at all. Our casualties were due to the intensity of the ground fighting in the South. We had already dropped a heavier tonnage of bombs than in all the theaters of World War II. During 1967, an estimated 90,000 North Vietnamese had infiltrated into South Viet Nam. In the opening weeks of 1968, infiltrators were coming in at three to four times the rate of a year earlier, despite the ferocity and intensity of our campaign of aerial interdiction.

In the wake of the Tet Offensive, Lyndon Johnson wearily reviews the text of a major televised address on Vietnam. The address, given on March 31, 1968, ended with his announcement that he would not seek a second full term as president—a surprise decision for which the Tet Offensive was largely responsible. (Courtesy of Corbis-Bettmann.)

"How long must we keep on sending our men and carrying the main burden of combat?" The South Vietnamese were doing better, but they were not ready yet to replace our troops and we did not know when they would be.

When I asked for a presentation of the military plan for attaining victory in Viet Nam, I was told that there was no plan for victory in the historic American sense. Why not? Because our forces were operating under three major political restrictions: The President had forbidden the invasion of North Viet Nam because this could trigger the mutual assistance pact between North Viet Nam and China; the President had forbidden the mining of the harbor at Haiphong, the principal port through which the North received military supplies, because a Soviet vessel might be sunk; the President had forbidden our forces to pursue the enemy into Laos and Cambodia, for to do so would spread the war, politically and geographically, with no discernible advantage. These and other restrictions which precluded an all-out, no-holds-barred military effort were wisely designed to prevent our being drawn into a larger war. We had no inclination to recommend to the President their cancellation.

"Given these circumstances, how can we win?" We would, I was told, continue to evidence our superiority over the enemy; we would continue to attack in the belief that he would reach the stage where he would find it inadvisable to go on with the war. He could not afford the attrition we were inflicting on him. And we were improving our posture all the time.

I then asked, "What is the best estimate as to how long this course of action will take? Six months? One year? Two years?" There was no agreement on an answer. Not only was there no agreement, I could find no one willing to express any confidence in his guesses. Certainly, none of us was willing to assert that he could see "light at the end of the tunnel" or that American troops would be coming home by the end of the year.

After days of this type of analysis, my concern had greatly deepened. I could not find out when the war was going to end; I could not find out the manner in which it was going to end; I could not find out whether the new requests for men and equipment were going to be enough, or whether it would take more and, if more, when and how much; I could not find out how soon the South Vietnamese forces would be ready to take over. All I had was the statement, given with too little self-assurance to be comforting, that if we persisted for an indeterminate length of time, the enemy would choose not to go on.

And so I asked, "Does anyone see any diminution in the will of the enemy after four years of our having been there, after enormous casualties and after massive destruction from our bombing?"

The answer was that there appeared to be no diminution in the will of the enemy. . . .

And so, after these exhausting days, I was convinced that the military course we were pursuing was not only endless, but hopeless. A further substantial increase in American forces could only increase the devastation and the Americanization of the war, and thus leave us even further from our goal of a peace that would permit the people of South Viet Nam to fashion their own political and economic institutions. Henceforth, I was also convinced, our primary goal should be to level off our involvement, and to work toward gradual disengagement.

Partly as a result of these meetings, Johnson soon decided against a major increase in the military effort in Vietnam. Instead he suspended the bombing of North Vietnam and began to pursue peace negotiations with the North Vietnamese and Viet Cong. (These dragged on for several years, with little result until the 1973 Paris Peace Accords.) With his popularity at an all-time low, Johnson also declared that he would not run for a second term as president. From then on, he and his successor, Richard Nixon, worked toward disengaging the United States from the "quagmire" in Vietnam.

Questions

1. *Compare the views of Gen. Westmoreland and Peter Braestrup on the American press corps during the Tet Offensive. Whose perspective do you find more persuasive and why?*
2. *The German military philosopher Carl von Clausewitz maintained that in war the ultimate objective is to break the enemy's will to continue the struggle. Evaluate the Tet Offensive in this light. Did it break the American will to continue the struggle?*
3. *Did Secretary of Defense Clark Clifford ask the right questions in his reevaluation of America's involvement in Vietnam? Are there other questions you believe he ought to have asked as well?*
4. *Did American policymakers make the right decision in choosing to disengage gradually from Vietnam after Tet? What other courses were available to them? What would you have done?*

FURTHER READING

The best survey of America's involvement in Vietnam is George C. Herring, America's Longest War: The United States and Vietnam, 1950–1975 *(New York, 1986). Stanley Karnow,* Vietnam: A History *(New York, 1983) is a sound, readable treatment of the entire thirty-year conflict, prepared as a companion to the PBS television series of the same name. (The PBS series, available on video, is well worth watching.) Don Oberdorfer,* Tet! *(Garden City, New York, 1971) remains the best account of the pivotal Communist offensive.* After Tet: The Bloodiest Year in Vietnam *(New York, 1993), by Ronald H. Spector, cogently weaves together political and military developments to create an effective snapshot of the American war effort at its height. As secretary of defense under both Kennedy and Johnson, Robert S. McNamara contributed heavily to the flawed American policy in Vietnam. His memoir,* In Retrospect: The Tragedy and Lessons of Vietnam *(New York, 1995) describes, in heavily self-critical tones, how that policy evolved.* On Strategy: A Critical Analysis of the Vietnam War *(Novato, California, 1982), by Harry G. Summers, Jr., makes the case that the United States could have prevailed in Vietnam had it adopted a better strategy. Although marred by bias and a turgid style, Gabriel Kolko,* Anatomy of a War: Vietnam, the United States, and the Modern Historical Experience *(New York, 1985), best illuminates the Vietnamese Communist revolutionary movement; it is unyielding in its insistence that the United States could not possibly have won.*